Cloud Computing for Beginners

Cloud Computing for Beginners

AparnaRajesh Atmakuri
N. Nalini
M. I. Thariq Hussan

CWP
Central West Publishing

Disclaimer
Every effort has been made by the publisher, authors while preparing this book, however, no warranties are made regarding the accuracy and completeness of the content. The publisher and authors disclaim without any limitation all warranties as well as any implied warranties about sales, along with fitness of the content for a particular purpose. Citation of any website and other information sources does not mean any endorsement from the publisher and authors. For ascertaining the suitability of the contents contained herein for a particular lab or commercial use, consultation with the subject expert is needed. In addition, while using the information and methods contained herein, the practitioners and researchers need to be mindful for their own safety, along with the safety of others, including the professional parties and premises for whom they have professional responsibility. To the fullest extent of law, the publisher and authors are not liable in all circumstances (special, incidental, and consequential) for any injury and/or damage to persons and property, along with any potential loss of profit and other commercial damages due to the use of any methods, products, guidelines, procedures contained in the material herein.

NATIONAL LIBRARY OF AUSTRALIA

A catalogue record for this book is available from the National Library of Australia

ISBN (print): 978-1-925823-95-0

About Authors

Mrs. AparnaRajesh Atmakuri has worked in various prestigious institutions across India. Currently, she is pursuing her doctorate in computer science. She has 15 years of teaching experience, with 8 international journal publications. She has presented papers in 15 international conferences and attended 12 seminars/workshops/FDP/QIP. She has published 2 books and attended workshop on High Impact Teaching Skills by Dale Carnegie Associates and Wipro Mission 10X.

Dr. N. Nalini is a Professor in the Department of Computer Science and Engineering at Nitte Meenakshi Institute of Technology, Bangalore. She has more than 24 years of teaching and 17 years of research experience. She has numerous international journal and conference publications to her credit, and received "Bharath Jyoti Award" by India International Friendship Society, New Delhi in 2012, from Dr. Bhishma Narain Singh, former Governor of Tamilnadu and Assam. She received the "Dr. Abdul Kalam Life Time Achievement National Award" for excellence in Teaching, Research Publications and Administration by International Institute for Social and Economic Reforms, IISER, Bangalore on 29th Dec 2014. She is also the recipient of "Distinguished Professor" award by TechNext India 2017 in association with Computer Society of India-CSI, Mumbai Chapter and "Best Professor in Computer Science &Engineering" award by 26th Business School Affaire Dewang Mehta National Education Awards (Regional Round) on 5th September 2018, at Bangalore. She is a lifetime member of the ISTE, CSI, ACEEE and IIFS. She was elected unanimously as Vice Chairman cum Chairman Elect of the Computer Society of India-Bangalore Chapter for the years 2019-2021.

Dr. M. I. Thariq Hussan is working as a Professor and Head, Department of Information Technology in Guru Nanak Institutions Technical Campus, Hyderabad, India. He has published 28 international journal publications. He has presented papers in 31 international/national conferences and attended 41 seminars/workshops/FDP/QIP. He has published 4 books and filed 3 patents. He has received Dedicated Professor and Best Teacher Award from reputed societies. He has qualified ESOL certificate in English by Cambridge University. He is a life member of ISTE and nominee member of CSI.

Contents

Preface

.

Preface

Cloud computing is an extraordinary worldview that empowers versatile, advantageous, on-request admittance to a shared pool of configurable computing and systems administration assets, for productively conveying applications and administrations over the Internet. For organizations, right now utilizing conventional frameworks, a cloud will empower clients to burn-through IT assets in the server farm in manners that were never accessible. The cloud likewise gives a UI that permits both the client and the IT overseer to effortlessly deal with the provisioned assets through the existence pattern of the administration demand. After a client's assets have been conveyed by a cloud, the client can track the request, which ordinarily comprises of some number of workers and programming, and see the wellbeing of those assets; add workers; change the introduced programming; eliminate workers; increment or abatement the designated handling force, memory or capacity; and indeed, even beginning, stop and restart servers.

An attempt has been made to write this book with simple topics that are of interest from beginners' perspective, academicians and new researchers who want to peruse their interest in cloud computing. It contains 10 chapters that follow a standard (learning objectives, introduction, number of diagrams, summary and references for further understanding) for easy understanding:

Chapter:1 Introduction to Cloud Computing
Chapter 2: Cloud Computing Architecture
Chapter 3: Cloud Computing Services
Chapter 4: Cloud Operating System
Chapter 5: Management in Cloud Computing
Chapter 6: Cloud and Virtualization
Chapter 7: Cloud Security
Chapter 8: Planning and Disaster Recovery in Cloud Computing
Chapter 9: Setting Up Own Cloud
Chapter 10: Future Directions

This book reflects the authors' lectures and research on some of the topics in cloud computing. Finally, the authors would like to thank Central West Publishing Australia for constant communication and support throughout the process of getting the book into print.

1

Introduction to Cloud Computing

Learning Objectives

- Understanding the cloud from business perspective, its evolution.
- Give an insight about cloud and virtualization
- Have a brief understanding on characteristics, advantages and disadvantages of cloud.
- To define building blocks of cloud.
- Provide an overview of technologies used for cloud and applications using cloud.
- Understanding issues related to cloud.

Distributed computing was authored for what happens when applications and administrations are moved into the web cloud. Cloud registering isn't something that all of a sudden seemed medium-term; in some structure, it might follow back to when PC frameworks remotely time-shared processing assets and applications. All the more presently however, distributed computing alludes to the various kinds of administrations and applications being conveyed in the web cloud, and the way that, as a rule, the gadgets used to get to these administrations and applications don't require any uncommon applications.

Computing in terms of cloud has seen an amazing development as of late. The essential inspiration for this development has been the guarantee of diminished capital and working costs, and the simplicity of progressively scaling and conveying new administrations without keeping up a dedicated infrastructure. Subsequently, distributed computing has started to quickly change the manner in which associations see their IT assets. From a situation of a solitary framework comprising of single working framework and single application, associations have been moving into cloud computing, where assets are accessible in plenitude and the client has a wide range to look over. Cloud computing is a model for empowering helpful, on-request system access to a mutual pool of configurable processing assets that can be quickly provisioned and discharged

1

with specialist co-op collaboration or negligible administration exertion.

In other way round, Cloud computing is a figuring worldview, where a huge pool of frameworks are associated in private or open systems, to give powerfully adaptable foundation to application, information and document stockpiling. With the appearance of this innovation, the expense of calculation, application facilitating, content stockpiling and conveyance is diminished fundamentally. Cloud computing is a useful way to deal with experience direct money saving advantages and it can possibly change a server farm from a capital-serious set up to a variable evaluated condition. Cloud figuring depends on an exceptionally basic head of reusability of IT abilities. The distinction that distributed computing brings contrasted with conventional ideas of "network registering", "disseminated processing", "utility figuring", or "autonomic processing" is to expand skylines crosswise over authoritative limits. Forrester characterizes distributed computing as: A pool of preoccupied, exceptionally adaptable, and oversaw figure framework fit for facilitating end client applications and charged by utilization.

Why Cloud Computing?

The importance of cloud computing is that it gives more adaptability than its past partners. It has indicated numerous advantages to big business IT world. Cost streamlining among them is the leader, since the guideline of cloud is pay as peruse. The added advantages are expanded versatility, convenience, most extreme able usage of assets, transportability of application, and so forth. This implies clients will probably get to data from anyplace whenever effectively without squandering the fundamental equipment assets perfect or unused. Because of its advantage, the present figuring innovation has seen a huge movement of 5 associations from their conventional IT foundation to cloud.

Some outstanding models incorporate the accompanying:

- Google - Has a private cloud that it utilizes for conveying Google Docs and numerous different administrations to its clients, including email get to, archive applications, content interpretations, maps, web examination, and substantially more.

- Microsoft - Has Microsoft Office 365 online administration that takes into account substance and business knowledge instruments to be moved into the cloud and Microsoft presently makes its office applications accessible in a cloud.
- Salesforce.com - Runs its application set for its clients in a cloud, and it's Force.com and Vmforce.com items furnish engineers with stages to construct altered cloud administrations.

Here, the end-clients need not to know the subtleties of a particular innovation while facilitating their application, as the administration is totally overseen by the Cloud Service Provider (CSP). Clients can expend administrations at a rate that is set by their specific needs. This on-request administration can be given whenever. CSP would deal with all the vital complex activities for the benefit of the client. It would give the total framework which dispenses the required assets for execution of client applications and the board of the whole framework 2 streams. Investigators state that pooling of assets and offices can help cut critical expenses for an organization.

Business and IT Perspective

Activated by the dynamic reception of the Cloud computing worldview in the IT administration advertise the IT reappropriating industry goes into a condition of motion. This discovers its appearance in the change of the customary provisioning model in IT redistributing where IT assets are physically situated at the customer's or seller's site. The idea of IT proficiency likewise grasps the thoughts epitomized in green processing, since not exclusively are the registering assets utilized all the more effectively, however further, the PCs can be physically situated in geological territories that approach modest power while their figuring force can be gotten to long separations away over the Internet. In any case, as the term business readiness suggests, distributed computing isn't just about shabby processing - it is likewise about organizations having the option to utilize computational instruments that can be sent and scaled quickly, even as it lessens the requirement for enormous forthright speculations that portray undertaking IT arrangements today. In thinking of our definition, we attempted to exemplify the key advantages of distributed computing from a business point of view just as its special highlights from a mechanical viewpoint.

Our formal meaning of cloud computing is as per the following: It is a data innovation administration model where registering administrations (both equipment and programming) are conveyed on-request to clients over a system in a self-administration style, autonomous of gadget and area. The assets required to give the essential quality-of service levels are shared, powerfully versatile, quickly provisioned, virtualized and discharged with insignificant specialist organization connection. Clients pay for the administration as a working cost without acquiring any huge beginning capital consumption, with the cloud administrations utilizing a metering framework that partitions the processing asset in suitable squares. The below figure demonstrates a schematic of the cloud computing model. It demonstrates how the registering assets in the cloud can be gotten to from an assortment of stages through the internet.

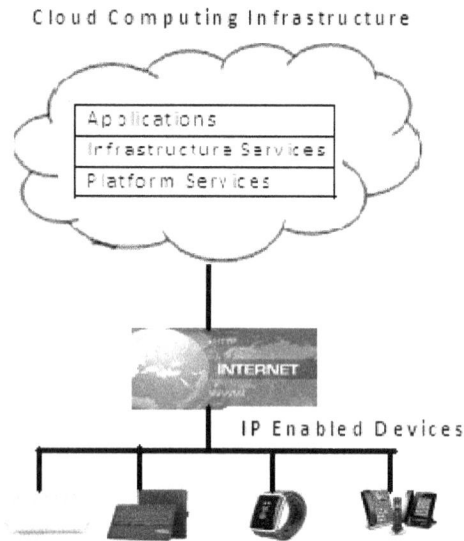

Figure 1. Basic idea of cloud infrastructure.

In particular, cloud computing offers the accompanying key points of interest in terms of business perspective:

- It significantly brings down the expense of section for littler firms attempting to profit by figure serious business investigation that were until now accessible just to the biggest of enterprises.

4

- The cloud turns into a versatile foundation that can be shared by various end clients, every one of whom may utilize it in altogether different ways. The clients are totally isolated from one another, and the adaptability of the framework.
- Cloud computing can bring down IT hindrances to advancement, as can be seen from the many promising new businesses, from the pervasive online applications, for example, Facebook and Youtube to the more engaged applications like TripIt or Mint.
- Cloud computing makes it simpler for endeavours to scale their administrations which are progressively dependent on precise data as indicated by customer request.
- Cloud computing likewise makes conceivable new classes of uses and conveys administrations that were impractical previously.

Built-up Players	Key Innovation Suppliers	The Pioneers
IBM gives distributed computing administrations called Blue Cloud, which offers organizations access to instruments that enable them to oversee enormous scale applications and database through IBM's Cloud	Apache's Hadoop is an open-source programming structure that has propelled the advancement of database and programming apparent uses for cloud computing. Incredible sponsor like IBM, Facebook, Yahoo also make Hadoop an impressive advancement environment for cloud computing applications	Amazon offers its Amazon Web Services, a suite of a few administrations which incorporate the Elastic Compute Cloud (EC2), for registering limit, and the Simple Storage Service (S3), for on-request stockpiling limit. Not with standing these center contributions, Amazon offers the SimpleDB (a database web administration), the CloudFront (a web administration for substance conveyance) and the Simple Queue Service (a facilitated administration for putting away messages as they travel between hubs)
Google's App Engine	EMC provides two	SalesForce.com is the

offers customer association's access to Google's cloud based stage that gives devices to fabricate and host web applications. Google Apps is rushing the business move from bundled programming to Web-facilitated administrations, and App Engine gives a valid option in the stage as an administration advertise	key segments in cloud computing capacity and virtualization programming. It is likewise coordinating a great deal of assets towards its distributed computing activities	main surely understood and fruitful SaaS application. Riding on its coat tails, the organization has now presented Force.com, a coordinated arrangement of instruments and application benefits that autonomous programming sellers and corporate IT divisions can use to fabricate any business application and run it on a similar framework that conveys the Salesforce CRM applications.
Microsoft organization has scheduled Windows Azure, the cloud working framework PaaS to show up in mid 2010. The Azure services platform to keep running on the Windows Azure working frameworks giving customer associations access to a few online Microsoft administrations like Live, .Net, SQL, SharePoint, and Microsoft's Dynamic CRM	Cisco - A generally late participant in the distributed computing space. Cisco is effectively taking a shot at a lot of norms that will permit convenience crosswise over suppliers. One significant part of that work is guaranteeing remaining task at hand movability starting with one self-governing framework then onto the next, which incorporates the predictable execution of the outstanding task at hand on the new framework	Anomaly's Elastic Computing Platform (ECP) coordinates venture server farms with business distributed computing contributions, allowing IT to experts oversee and administer both inward and outer assets from a solitary support, while making it simple to move virtual machines starting with one server farm then onto the next
AT&T gives two cloud administrations: Synaptic Hosting, through which cus-		

tomer organizations will most likely store Windows serve, Linux customer server applications and web applications on AT&T's cloud Synaptic Storage, empowering customers to store their information on AT&T's cloud.		

Cloud Computing as Evolution of Internet

The idea of cloud computing goes back to the 1960s with thoughts, for example, the intergalactic PC arrange, presented by J.C.R. Licklider while introducing ARPANET through an update to the logical community. The idea of a cloud didn't exist around then; however it was the introduction of the internet and the reflection of the systems administration layer that brought forth the idea of a unique way between various PC frameworks. Very little later, John McCarthy proposed that processing may some time or another be composed as an open utility similarly as the phone framework is an open utility while talking at MIT's centennial festival in 1961. He likewise portrayed the potential for this innovation as a framework where every supporter needs to pay just for the limit he really utilizes, yet he approaches all programming dialects normal for an exceptionally enormous framework. Certain endorsers may offer administration to other endorsers. The PC utility could turn into the bases of another and significant industry. These words prophetically portray what we're encountering today in present day cloud computing.

By and by, it wasn't until a lot after when cloud computing progressed toward becoming standard at the point when organizations, for example, Salesforce.com spearheaded the conveyance of big business frameworks. Salesforce conveyed their product by utilizing another methodology, rather than charging clients to purchase a product permit forthright, they would charge through a month to month membership model. By utilizing this model, it wound up conceivable to get to programming facilitated remotely through a basic site that could scale contingent upon the use and would be charged in comparable design. The most significant achievement for current cloud processing was the dispatch of EC2, the Elastic Compute Cloud created by Amazon Web Services, and what later turned into the outline for Infrastructure-as-a-Service (IaaS).

IaaS permitted people also, little organizations to lease PCs on which they would run their applications by paying just for the assets that they utilized continuously with the guarantee that they would almost certainly scale in size at some random point with essentially boundless limit. This ability was at that point bolstered inside using virtualization, yet customarily caused in capital consumptions with huge starting ventures and lower upkeep expenses. Amazon had an ambitious start in the IaaS market, and they were for all intents and purposes alone in that market for quite a while, yet it wasn't a lot after that different organizations, for example, Rackspace entered with comparative item contributions, and in the long run Microsoft and Google gotten up to speed in 2010 and 2012 separately.

What is Cloud Computing?

To be sure, in the data innovation business there is no understanding on what cloud computing truly infers, and some industry heavyweights and intellectuals consider the term careless and have been energetically limited to its usage. The web itself has usually been depicted as a cloud in system outlines, and, much equivalent to the web, business customers don't need to recognizing what way it capacities, they as of late need to grasp what they can do with it. There is something else entirely to cloud computing than brilliant innovation; to data innovation buyers it addresses a significantly assorted technique for getting a full reach out of data innovation abilities on a compensation for each usage establishment. At a central level when you use a PC you speak with three layers of registering. As a matter of first importance, at the most diminished layer, you have a physical piece of equipment with its processors, memory chips, plate drives, arrange cards and various parts - the specialist can call this the framework. Second, in the middle layer, you have a working structure, (for instance Microsoft Windows) that interfaces with the equipment and outfits an unfaltering situation for running and propelling programming (using Visual Basic or Microsoft Access, for example). Moreover finally, at the top, there are substitute gathering programming applications, (for instance word changing packs) that you use in your work and play and can call this programming.

Cloud computing alludes to controlling, designing, and getting to the applications on the web. It offers online information stockpiling, framework and application.

Cloud computing is a worldview of appropriated figuring to give the clients on-request, utility-based processing administrations. Cloud clients can give progressively dependable, accessible and refreshed administrations to their customers thus. Cloud itself comprises of physical machines in the server farms of cloud suppliers. Virtualization is given over these physical machines. These virtual machines are given to the cloud clients. Distinctive cloud supplier gives cloud administrations of various reflection levels. For example Amazon EC2 empowers the clients to deal with extremely low level subtleties where Google App-Engine gives an improvement stage to the designers to build up their applications. So the cloud administrations are partitioned into numerous sorts like Software as a Service, Platform as a Service or Infrastructure as a Service. These administrations are accessible over the Internet in the entire reality where the cloud goes about as the single purpose of access for serving all clients. Cloud computing design tends to troubles of enormous scale information handling.

History of Cloud Computing

The idea of cloud computing isn't new. Truth is told, quite a bit of what we do on our PCs today require it. What is changing is the manner in which that we see what cloud computing can really accomplish for us today. The power and size of the cloud has changed enormously from what it was before all else. After some time as the innovation and business conditions had advanced, the norm of cloud computing has changed. What was known as cloud computing quite a while in the past was the equivalent on a fundamental level, yet the utilizations in data today have changed by a tremendous degree. In any case, there is no uncertainty that this sort of preparing force is for sure winding up progressively common by bigger organizations that have a practically insatiable hunger for the capacity to process errands, for example, doing the math and giving clients with Web 2.0 usefulness. Increasingly more data is out there in the advanced domain and there is such a large amount of it that should be composed in manners that we can completely get it and use to further our potential benefit.

The start of what is known as the idea of cloud computing can be followed back to the centralized computer days of the 1960s when the possibility of utility registering was instituted by MIT PC researcher and Turing grant champ John McCarthy. Later in 1969 J. C. R. Licklider, a PC researcher, created ARPANET (Advanced Research Projects Agency Network) the immediate antecedent to the web. His vision was for everybody to be interconnected and getting to projects and information at any site, (particularly like distributed computing). Mid 1970s marked the accessibility of full time-sharing on stages such as Multics (on GE equipment), Cambridge CTSS, and the soonest UNIX ports (on DEC equipment). It was in the late 1990s that organizations, for example, Sun Microsystems started touting what appeared at the time the showcasing idea that the system is the PC. Or on the other hand the possibility that oracle author Larry Ellison (who later put resources into Salesforce.com) had for terminal machines that would cost under $300. These thoughts were in fact significant, yet they never truly took off as shoppers were searching for increasingly complete PC arrangements that had, for instance, some stockpiling limit accessible. By and by, it wasn't until a lot after when cloud registering progressed toward becoming standard at the point when organizations, for example, Salesforce.com spearheaded the conveyance of big business frameworks. Salesforce conveyed their product by utilizing another methodology, rather than charging clients to purchase a product permit forthright, they would charge through a month to month membership model. By utilizing this model, it ended up conceivable to get to programming facilitated remotely through a basic site that could scale contingent upon the use and would be charged in comparable style to a utility. These organizations moved toward becoming intermediaries of cloud registering to their clients, yet didn't offer real foundation that could be utilized for a nonexclusive reason. Below is the figure for cloud inception in different organizations.

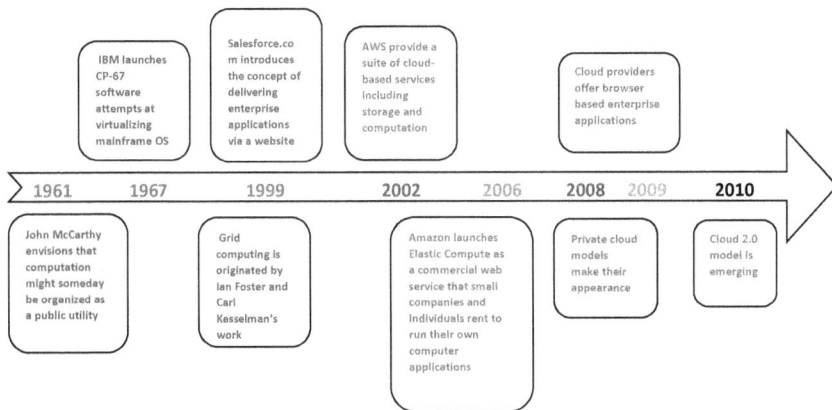

Figure 2. History of cloud computing.

Cloud and Virtualization

In computing, virtualization is the way toward abstracting processing assets such that various applications can share solitary physical equipment. Put in an unexpected way, virtualization alludes to the making of a virtual, as opposed to real, rendition of an asset. The standard case of virtualization is server virtualization, in which certain properties of a physical server are decoupled (disconnected) and recreated in a hypervisor (virtualization programming) as vCPU, vRAM, vNIC, and so on.; these are at that point amassed subjectively to deliver a virtual server, in a couple of moments seconds. Processing assets are by all account not the only assets that are virtualized; stockpiling can be virtualized as well. Through virtualization it is possible that one asset is shared among numerous clients or various assets, e.g., stockpiles, are accumulated and introduced as one or all the more high limit asset that can be utilized by one or numerous clients. In any of those cases, the client has the fantasy of sole possession. Other than figuring and capacity, a system might be virtualized as well. That is, the thought of reflection can be reached out from figuring assets and capacity to the central segments of the systems, i.e., hubs and connections. Thusly, in a more extensive setting, virtualization alludes to the production of a virtual form of an asset, for example, a working framework, a capacity gadget, or system assets. Server and work area virtualization is an experienced innovation now. Virtualization programming, e.g., VMware Workstation maps the physical equipment assets to the virtual machines

11

that embody a working framework and its applications, as appeared in figure below. Each virtual machine completely likeness a standard x86 machine, as it has its very own focal handling unit (CPU), memory, disks, and I/O gadgets.

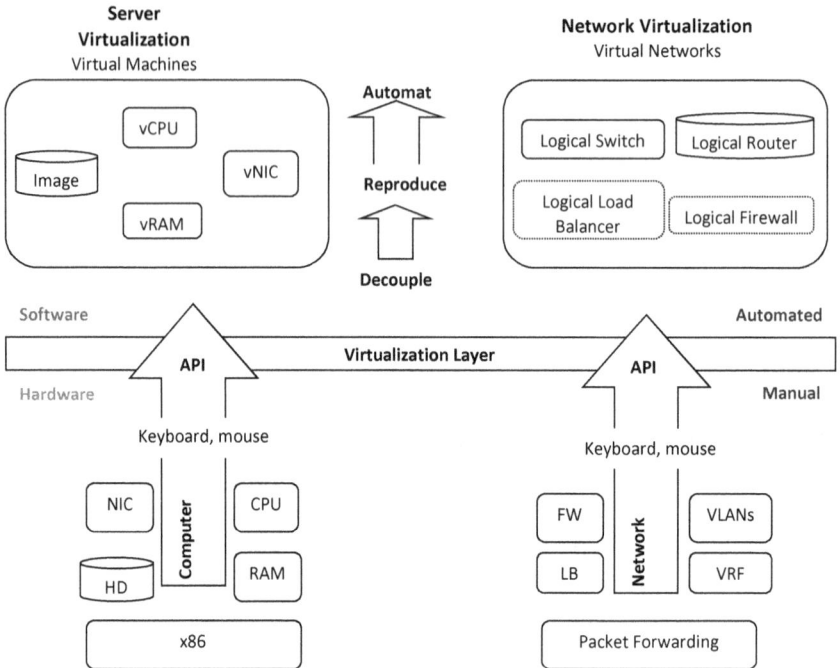

Figure 3. Cloud and virtualization.

Why Virtualization?

The basic motivation for virtualization is to efficiently share resources among multiple users. This is similar to multitasking operating systems where, rather than doing one task at a time, unused computing power is used to run another task.

The essential inspiration for virtualization is to productively share assets among various clients. This is like performing various tasks working frameworks where, as opposed to completing one assignment at once, unused figuring force is utilized to run another errand. Consider an association that has numerous servers all doing single or a little group of related errands. Without losing the security of secluded conditions, virtualization enables these servers to be supplanted by a solitary physical machine which has a number of virtual servers. Additionally, storage accumulation upgrades the general sensibility of capacity and gives better sharing of storage assets. Relocation is another huge favorable position of virtualization. It proves to be useful if an update is required or when the equipment is defective on the grounds that it is genuinely basic to migrate a virtual machine from one physical machine to another. Therefore, expanding reinforcement ability is another convincing purpose behind virtualization. In the event that a server crashes, the information on that server can be set to be consequently moved to another server in the system. Saving money on physical machine costs, decreased vitality utilization, and littler physical space prerequisite are among other prominent points of interest of virtualization.

The cloud decides how those virtualized assets are distributed, conveyed, and exhibited. Virtualization isn't important to make a cloud situation; however, it empowers quick scaling of assets in a manner that nonvirtualized conditions discover hard to accomplish. At this point the user ought to have understood the association among virtualization and Cloud computing. Extensively, these two innovations share a typical bond: they are both intended to expand efficiencies and diminish costs. They are very unique however. Virtualization is one of the components that structures cloud computing. It is the programming that controls equipment, while cloud computing is an administration that outcomes from that control .Seeing that distributed computing is based on a virtualized framework, one can deduct that if an association have just put resources into virtualization, they may bring in cloud to further expand the registering effectiveness. At that point, the cloud could deal with top of the current virtualized framework; it likewise helps in the conveyance of current organize as an administration. Put in an unexpected way, distributed computing utilizes virtualized assets at an alternate level, where the assets can be gotten to as an administration, and in an on-request way. On the other hand, any association considering reception of a private cloud must take a shot at virtualization, too Organizations can improve the processing assets productivity through virtualization; The path from virtualization to a self-administration cloud presents specialized just as authoritative moves identified with the executives and operational procedures, culture, and legislative issues. The accompanying five stages fill in as a structure to enable you to comprehend and effectively address the authoritative and innovation issues you will confront. Ignoring any of these can entangle you and cause your venture to fall flat. The system:

Stage 1: **Develop a cloud strategy** - A cloud procedure obviously expresses the advantages, approach, and expected results for your innovation speculation over your association.

Stage 2: **Manage business process change** - Business procedure changes are inescapable in a cloud usage. For your cloud undertaking to succeed, you should team up with procedure proprietors to precisely report the procedures and errands influenced and decide how to limit the quantity of required human control focuses.

Stage 3: **Numerous clients** in huge organizations are as of now acquainted with the idea of devouring IT administrations. Sorting out your IT workforce around cloud administration conveyance empowers you to serve the business all the more viably as a cloud administrations representative.

Stage 4: **Put the right technology in place** - Your cloud won't prevail without the correct innovation. Set your innovation needs dependent on the usage stages and achievements portrayed in your cloud methodology.

Stage 5: **Manage a data-driven cloud** - End-to-end wellbeing and execution checking of the environment is fundamental for cloud the executives. Without information accumulation and investigation, you won't have the data you have to profit by framework efficiencies or measure achievement.

Characteristics of Cloud Computing

Cloud computing rises as one of the sultriest points in the field of data innovation. Cloud computing depends on a few other registering research territories, for example, HPC, virtualization, utility figuring and network processing. So as to clarify the fundamental of distributed computing, we propose the qualities of this zone which make distributed computing being distributed computing and recognize it from other research regions. The distributed computing has its very own conceptional, specialized, financial and client experience attributes. This segment breaks down these qualities and distinguishes the notable highlights of each to decide the job that they may play in your organization's relocation to the cloud.

On-request self-administration: The primary trademark is one of the most effortless to characterize. It basically requires these two things to be valid:

- The administration must be constantly accessible (or some sensible guess of consistently).
- The administration got must be modifiable by the customer association without reaching the facilitating supplier.

Wide system access: In this specific situation, wide system access implies that the facilitated application ought to be reachable by means of about any network based machine. These can incorporate, however are not constrained to the accompanying: Laptop, Desktop, Smartphone and Tablet gadget wide system access is regularly practiced by utilizing the inherent internet browser for the gadget, as it is one of the most universal customers accessible.

Asset pooling: Asset pooling / Resource pooling is the idea that different associations can share the hidden physical cloud framework. This permits essentially more noteworthy buying power for these organizations since they can ordinarily acquire access to a bigger pool of assets instead of getting the physical or virtual framework themselves.

Fast flexibility: This is the capacity to deal with spikes in use at any rate semi automatically. While this is something you could in fact acquire with physical equipment, the turnaround time essential for execution normally pushes that arrangement outside the limits of the meaning of quick.

Metered use: Metered utilization is additionally a clear thought: you just pay the facilitating supplier for the assets you expend. This makes IT all the more an utility administration you pay for instead of the customary cost models, where you may pay some dollar figure a month to have X number of servers. Basically, metered utilization might be the idea of $X every moment or hour your server is fuelled on and this is the means by which most open cloud suppliers work.

Advantages of Cloud Computing

Low cost - Entering the cloud is a minimal effort suggestion. It doesn't require an enormous capital speculation in advance for equipment, hardware and foundation. You should have work areas, workstations or some sort of gadget to get to the Internet and use your information. The most ideal approach to think about the expense of cloud computing is to think as far as leasing versus owning. The cloud supplier possesses and keeps up the majority of the assets and the business customer starts to utilize it for a month to month or yearly charge. This is like what is ordinarily alluded to as the Software-as-a-Service (or SaaS) model. This kind of model gives the entrepreneur greater consistency in planning for these expenses.

Extreme interest of intelligent applications - Applications with ongoing reaction and ability of giving data either by different clients or by nonhuman sensors increasing more today. These are by and large pulled in to cloud due to high accessibility as well as in light of the fact that these administrations are commonly information escalated and require investigating information crosswise over various sources.

Flexibility - With cloud computing, since you pay for what you use, you have the adaptability to just utilize what you need. This implies on the off chance that you are a private company in a start-up mode, you can begin little. Some cloud suppliers are set up to consequently scale for your asset requests. The framework can typically be tweaked to your needs. It very well may be a private system, open, or a mix of both. Also, the cloud bolsters multi-stage improvement situations.

Simple, fast, easy - The excellence of cloud computing is that it's simple. Utilizing cloud computing can streamline numerous pieces of your business. Your business can run all the more effectively when you tap into electronic applications that are accessible in the cloud. Everything from prospect the board applications to client charging and invoicing can be moved out of your shop and into the cloud. This enables you to concentrate on what you specialize in your business and exceed expectations at your qualities while another person handles the regulatory capacities.

Parallel cluster preparing - Cloud naturally supports clump handling and dissecting tera-bytes of information in all respects effectively. Programming models like Google's guide lessen and Yahoo's! open source partner Hadoop can be utilized to do these concealing operational multifaceted nature of parallel handling of many distributed computing servers.

Accessibility - Regardless of where you are on the planet, you can get to your cloud based applications. Gone is the muddled remote login techniques required for your in-house arrange. The main thing required is a gadget that can get to the web and an Internet association. This implies your staff can approach anyplace and at whenever, from home, office or out and about at a customer's office.

New pattern in business world and academic network - Lately the business endeavours are keen on finding client's needs, purchasing behaviors, and supply chains to take top administration choices. These require examination of exceptionally enormous measure of online information.

Sustainability - Should a cataclysmic event strike your business, fortunately your registering ability lives elsewhere? Clearly, this is a hindrance if the fiasco hits your cloud supplier.

Broad work area application - Some work area applications like MATLAB, Mathematica are winding up so process escalated that a solitary work area machine is never again enough to run them. So they are created to be equipped for utilizing cloud computing to perform broad assessments

Disadvantages of Cloud Computing

Security of data - This is one of the essential concerns identified with distributed computing. In an extremely essential sense, the information that used to live inside the four dividers of your office currently lives somewhere else. The security of that information must be tended to, especially if the information contains exchange mysteries, restrictive records, client documents, and so forth.

Redundancy - This term alludes to the unwavering quality of your online applications that keep running in the cloud. Suppose, be if the server that your site is running on accidents, another server gets the last known point of interest and your business continues onward. This is redundancy.

Policy concern - Government hosts certain arrangements however the third gathering cloud supplier may have repudiating strategies.

Costs when under attack - Even however cloud computing offers an extraordinary minimal effort alternative for independent companies, it can really cost more cash if an organization's site goes under a distributed denial of service (DDoS) attack. When the site is attacked, the supplier will just start to build the assets that the site requires (because of the assault) and bill for the assets gave. It is imperative to solicit the supplier what kind from arrangements they need to secure against this sort of assault.

Lack of confidence in systems - Many government divisions don't have that much trust in systems and web. So they would not bounce into tolerating cloud computing.

Performance can vary - In a cloud situation, your applications are running on servers that at the same time give assets to different organizations. As the prerequisites for different clients go here and there, the exhibition of a lot of the assets will fluctuate. Frequently, a cloud supplier may guarantee that the assets accessible to you are boundless. This might be hypothetically valid, however from a practical perspective the equipment adaptability is most likely restricted. You may not realize precisely how adaptable it is until you arrive at your utilization constraint on their framework.

Cloud Building Blocks

Cloud computing is made of three very important building blocks computing, networking and storage.

Computing: Computing is the core of the cloud advertising. It is offered as handling capacities controlled by virtual machines that keep running on a physical host server. There are a few factors that are a piece of a register offering: RAM, CPUs, Disk and Bandwidth. Normally, these four factors are consolidated to create various kinds of servers that address diverse calculation remaining tasks at hand.

While a large portion of the present register is accomplished through virtual machines, there are a few contributions accessible on exposed equipment, for example, AWS Lambda, a compute item that is planned to run occasion based capacities that are activated under specific conditions and that can spinoff the hidden virtual machines without requiring the client input. Another type of compute is accessible through PaaS contributions that run code without requiring the client to arrange or keep up the fundamental foundation.

Storage: Cloud suppliers regularly offer storage through various strategic block storages, content delivery networks and article stockpiling. Storage can be joined straightforwardly to the physical server as in conventional PC designs, yet it can likewise be connected to the virtual machine through block storage or volumes.

Networking: Systems administration incorporates an enormous number of items including domain name system (DNS), subnet creation capacities, sharing of Internet Protocol addresses (IPs), Virtual Land Area Networks (VLANs) and the transmission capacity important to associate the various bits of the foundation, explicitly virtual machines and storage arrangements.

Which Technologies are Used?

Cloud computing systems utilized various technologies some of which are, data storage, data management, virtualization and parallel programming model.

Data storage: As to guarantee high validity and economy, cloud computing receives appropriated storage to spare information, utilizing repetition storage to guarantee the unwavering quality of put away information and utilizing high tenable programming to make up the extraordinariness of the equipment, consequently giving the shabby and sound mass conveyed capacity and processing framework. The information storage arrangement of cloud computing are:

- Google File System (GFS) utilized in huge and appropriated applications which need to access mass information.
- Hadoop Distributed File System (HDFS) embrace Master/Slave design, a HDFS bunch makes up of a Namenode and a few Data hubs. Namenode is a middle server which is in

charge of dealing with the record framework namespace and the customer access to documents. Normally a hub has a datanode which is in charge of overseeing stockpiling of the hub.

Data management: Cloud computing needs to process and break down mass and circulated information, in this way, information the executive's innovation must most likely proficiently oversee huge informational indexes. There are two kinds of technologies in cloud computing framework:

- BigTable of Google
- HBase created by Hadoop group

Virtualization: Virtualization is a strategy for sending processing assets. It isolates the various degrees of the application framework including equipment, programming, information, systems administration, stockpiling, etc, breaks the division among the server farm, servers, stockpiling, systems administration, information and the physical gadgets, acknowledge dynamic engineering, and accomplishes the objectives of overseeing brought together and use progressively the physical assets and virtual assets, improving the adaptability of the framework, diminishing the cost, improving the administration and lessening the danger of the executives.

Parallel programming model: To empower clients proficiently to utilize cloud computing assets and all the more effectively appreciate administrations that cloud figuring achieves; cloud computing programming model must make assignment booking and parallel execution straightforward to clients and software engineers. Cloud computing embraces MapReduce programming model, which breaks down the assignment into numerous subtasks, and through two stages (Map and Reduce) to acknowledge planning and portion in the huge scale hub. MapReduce is a parallel programming framework created by Google. It puts parallelism and deficiency resistance, information appropriation, and burden balance in a database, and every one of the activities of information are condensed in two stages: Map and Reduce.

What kind of Applications can use Cloud Computing?

Applications of cloud computing is one of the most prevailing field of registering assets online on the grounds that sharing and the management of assets is simple utilizing cloud. These properties have made it a functioning segment in the accompanying fields as pursues:

Marketing companies: Cloud computing promotes companies to a new level. The dealer can have a commercial centre without the need of putting resources into additional equipment, programming, permit expenses and so on and the purchaser has more alternatives for items. Cloud processing is changing the manner in which marketing completes today. Purchasers are investing a greater amount of their energy web based, scanning for data, cooperating with similar associates and companions over cloud-based informal communities and having their very own substance facilitated in the cloud. Offline marketing methods keep on plunging in their adequacy, even as new cloud-enhanced marketing techniques, for example, web based life; paid pursuit and site improvement convey both short and long haul results

Online personal media store: Individuals presently attempt to keep every one of their media in advanced arrangement. They store it on hard circles, CDs, DVDs and BDs. Be that as it may, despite everything it shapes a massive gathering with the opportunity of losing their information continually waiting over their psyche. Consider the possibility that they had a personal media store on the cloud. Imagine a scenario where they can utilize their Televisions to store all they need on the cloud. This can be conceivable. TVs associated with the Internet can be utilized to dump all the individual media on the cloud. The cloud would then be able to sort and arrange the media under different classifications and make an accessible list of all the client content. This information would then be able to be altered by the showcase and different capacities of all the user's gadgets.

E-learning: It is another pattern in the field of instruction that gives an alluring situation to students, employees, and specialists. Students, employees, scientists can associate with the haze of their association and access information and data from that point.

Medical fields: Within an emergency clinic, without a doubt inside most of restorative practices, understanding graphs and medicinal accounts are regularly kept inside a PC arrangement or the like. In a clinic this is particularly valuable as the sheer number of patients inside the structure at any one time can be devastating. Cloud computing can help encourage simpler access and conveyance of data among the different therapeutic experts who may interact with every individual patient. In current immense emergency clinics, servers are associated, yet the sheer measure of data and PCs that must be associated is stunning. A cloud-based framework will improve data sharing by permitting everything to be facilitated in a similar spot, enabling a specialist to info test brings about the lab, right away refreshing the outline of a patient in a totally discrete wing.

On demand gaming: Games are process serious applications. To such an extent that they have committed stages worked for genuine gamers. TVs also have in-constructed games yet not of the class of center games. This is on the grounds that center games require enormous figure control that Televisions can't give. Since Televisions have moved toward becoming web empowered, we can utilize the process intensity of the Cloud to do the calculation at the backend. We can push the gaming reassures on the cloud. All the client cooperation can be pushed onto the cloud; the cloud will process dependent on the game principles and send back the outcomes for the Television to show.

Enterprise resource planning (ERP): Use of cloud in ERP appears when the matter of any association develops. Crafted by overseeing applications, HR, finance and so on winds up costly and complex. To defeat it service providers can introduce ERP in the cloud itself.

E-governance: Cloud computing can improve the working of a legislature by improving the manner in which it gives the administrations to its natives, foundations and participation with different governments. This should be possible by growing the accessibility of condition, making condition progressively adaptable and tweaked. It likewise removed the weight of overseeing, introducing and redesigning applications.

Better research opportunities: Cloud computing in training opens roads for better research, discourse, and coordinated effort. It additionally gives a product work area condition, which limits equipment issues. Cloud computing likewise empowers classes to be kept running on remote areas. The advantages of cloud computing are that outside substances may be increasingly advanced at overseeing individual information. These substances might most likely oversee information more modestly and viably than the instructive organization could do itself.

Telecommunication: Cloud computing used for telecom industries known as cloud communication. Telecom organizations can utilize cloud computing to give both private and open cloud systems to clients and associations for local and business purposes. Cloud correspondences are internet-based voice and information interchanges where telecom applications, exchanging and storage are facilitated by a third-party outside of the association utilizing them, and they are accessed over the open internet.

Major Issues in Cloud Computing

Secured cloud computing uses the virtual processing, clients' personal information might be dispersed in different virtual server farms as opposed to remain in the equivalent physical area, clients may release shrouded data when they are accessing services of cloud computing.

Dependability - Sometimes the cloud servers may experience breakdown or slowdown as like our local server.

Lawful issues related worries stick with security measures and classification of individual entirely through authoritative levels. Numerous guidelines relating to the capacity and utilization of information require ordinary revealing and review of trails. Notwithstanding the necessities to which clients are subjected to, the server farms kept up by cloud suppliers may likewise be liable to consistence prerequisites.

Opportunity - Cloud processing does not enable clients to physically have the capacity of the information, leaving the information storage and control in the hands of cloud suppliers.

Long haul viability - One needs to make it certain that the information one puts into the cloud will never end up invalid even if the cloud supplier becomes penniless or get obtained and gobbled up by a bigger organization.

Summary

This chapter starts with the importance of cloud in today's business, and discusses how cloud and internet are related to each other. Cloud computing evolution, definition is also explained. Further several technologies and applications of cloud are elaborated. The chapter ends with detailed note on issues related to cloud computing.

References

1. NIST Definition of Cloud Computing- https://www.nist.gov/programsprojects/cloud-computing
2. [Available online] https://en.wikipedia.org/wiki/Cloud_computing
3. [Available online] https://www.salesforcetutorial.com/introduction-to-cloud-computing/
4. [Available online] https://www.w3schools.in/cloud-computing/history-of-cloud-computing/

Further readings

1. https://www.datapine.com/blog/cloud-computing-risks-and-challenges/
2. Y. Ghanam, J. Ferreira, F. Maurer, Emerging Issues and Challenges in Cloud Computing-A Hybrid Approach, Journal of Software Engineering and Applications, Vol. 5, No. 11A, 2012, Pages 923-937, DOI: 10.4236/jsea.2012.531107.
3. Sean Marston, Zhi Li, Subhajyoti Bandyopadhyay, Anand Ghalsasi, Cloud Computing - The Business Perspective, Decision Support Systems, Volume 1, Pages 1-11, 2011, DOI: 10.1109/HICSS.2011.102.

2

Cloud Computing Architecture

Learning Objectives

- Provide an overview of cloud computing stack.
- Describe the role of cloud sourcing in cloud computing.
- Provide an overview about service models.
- Give a detailed description of deployment models in cloud.

The term architecture starts from structure development where it alludes to the craftsmanship or routine with regards to planning and developing structures. While in standard terms it alludes to the artistic expression, this term basically too passes on how the usefulness is accomplished utilizing normal standards. In the realm of data innovation, it one of the parts isn't working appropriately long the entrance chain, the cloud execution will fall flat.

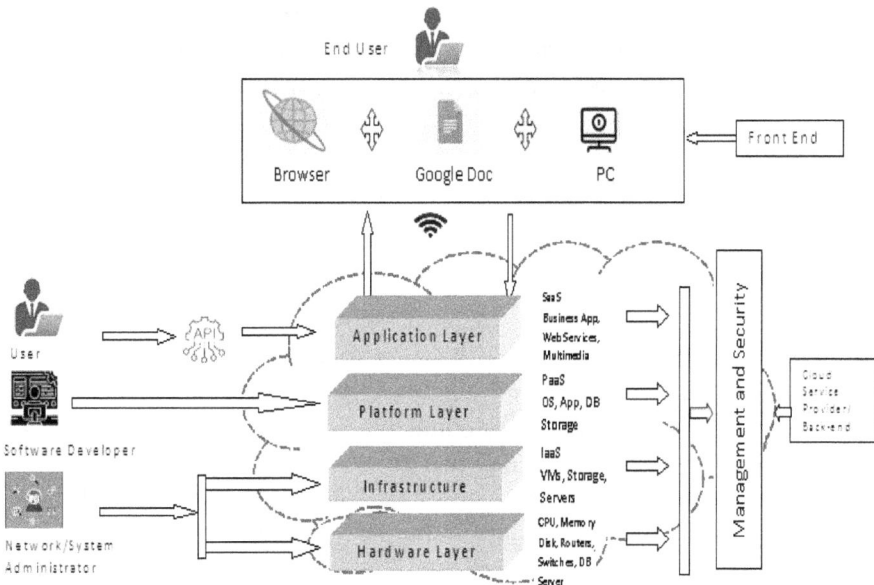

Figure 4. Cloud commuting architecture.

Cloud architecture envelops an assortment of frameworks and advances just as administration deploying, and business models. The blend of front-end services and back-end services complete the cloud architecture.

Front End

This design causes us to see, how the cloud processing assets are being shared by means of Front End. It is the noticeable interface to the clients, customers, and clients alongside the customer's organization empowered gadgets that are utilized to get to the cloud climate. Front end design is separated into three sections:

Internet browser - It empowers cloud figuring programming to run client terminal taking the essence of an internet browser or a customer application.

Google Doc - A client can straightforwardly collaborate with the cloud through UI by means of Gmail, Google Doc, or a content tool.

Customer PC and networks - These are associated a piece of Front end that incorporates client's PC and other information gadgets alongside web associations/to perform figuring on cloud.
Distinctive cloud registering framework uses various interfaces, you can look over the assortment of internet browsers, for example, Chrome, Safari, and Firefox alongside google docs. The front-end stage contains meagre and fat customers, tablets, and cell phones, where a large portion of the IT experts speak with one another and with clouds.

Back End

An Ideal backend design consistently enables its front end as it grasps the whole framework on the cloud. The cloud processing backend design is overseen by cloud specialist co-ops which are situated on far off workers. They are generally made out of an actual get together of six layers beginning from application, platform, foundation, infrastructure, hardware and security.

Application layer - Application layer is referred to as programming as an assistance which one of the crucial pieces of cloud is figuring engineering. This highest layer can be any product application or web administration upheld by SaaS that deals with the customer's solicitations and necessities. This Application layer is only the circulation model where an outsider hosts application and makes them accessible to clients over the web. SaaS eliminates costs and necessities of equipment, upkeep, permitting, establishment, and backing.

Platform layer - This layer involves OS and applications to give a PaaS stage to programming advancement and organization significant for consistent cloud figuring tasks.

Foundation layer - This layer incorporates capacity units (CPU, Motherboard, Graphics Processing Unit (GPU), VMs, virtualization programming, and workers on the IaaS stage that drives whole cloud programming administrations on host application and organization level. Framework administrators can get to this adaptable stockpiling and register power at whatever point required.

Infrastructure layer - This is the base most layer in cloud design, basically comprises of the multitude of perspectives that can be genuinely overseen, for example, information base worker, switches, switches, memory circle to control equipment setups, adaptation to internal failure alongside power flexibly and traffic the executives.

Hardware layer - The administration programming is utilized to designate assets to explicit assignments and deals with the consistent working of the cloud climate. It goes about as an arbiter that organizes among frontend and backend design in a cloud registering framework.

Security - Security is a basic segment of any cloud processing framework. Security keeps the troubleshooting cycle adjusted to adapt up to the security issues. To guarantee security in a cloud processing framework, normal stockpiling reinforcement is the initial step, though virtual firewalls are different components to keep up cloud security.

Cloud Computing Stack

Cloud computing is frequently depicted as a stack, as a reaction to the expansive scope of administrations based over each other under the moniker cloud. The by and large acknowledged meaning of cloud computing originates from the National Institute of Standards and Technology (NIST).

Cloud computing is a model for empowering helpful, on-request system access to a mutual pool of configurable processing that can be quickly provisioned and discharged with negligible administration exertion or specialist co-op communication. What this implies in plain terms is the capacity for end clients to use portions of mass assets and that these assets can be procured rapidly and effectively. NIST likewise offers up a few qualities that it sees as fundamental for a support of being considered "Cloud." These attributes include:

- On-request self-administration
- Broad system gets to
- Resource pooling
- Rapid flexibility
- Measured help

More than a semantic contention around classification, we accept that so as to expand the advantages that cloud computing brings an answer needs to show these specific qualities. This is particularly valid since as of late there has been a move by customary programming sellers to showcase arrangements as cloud computing which are commonly acknowledged to not fall inside the meaning of genuine cloud computing, a training known as cloud-washing.

The graph beneath delineates the cloud computing stack - it demonstrates three unmistakable classes inside cloud computing: Software as a Service, Platform as a Service and Infrastructure as a Service.

These sorts of cloud figuring portray precisely what a business can do with the cloud. The chart to the privilege exhibits what is known as the cloud processing stack. These are the three classes of cloud registering:

- SaaS applications are intended for end-clients, conveyed over the web.
- PaaS is the arrangement of instruments and administrations intended to make coding and sending those applications snappy and effective.

- IaaS is the equipment and programming that forces everything - servers, stockpiling, systems, working frameworks.

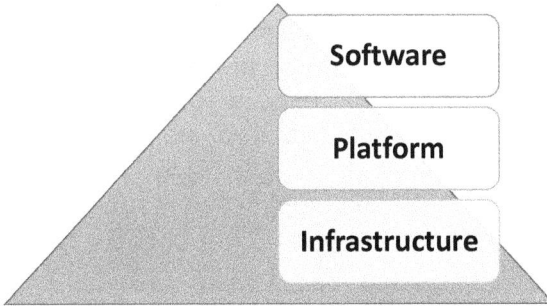

Figure 5. Cloud computing stack.

Cloud Sourcing

Cloud computing is anything but a mechanically new worldview. The center innovations fused in cloud computing model have been promptly accessible. For what reason is it then that previous day distributed computing developed today as cloud computing. To comprehend this reappearance, it is valuable to see reception and sending of data advances in associations in a more noteworthy point of view. During prior receptions of data innovations by associations, there has been an absence of composed longer-term procedure and arranging. Divisions inside the association, and their branches, have been conveying data frameworks meeting their particular needs. This has prompted various establishments having covering functionalities yet inadequate with regards to interoperability. Therefore, the executives and support expenses of data advances have risen pointedly. To decrease increasing costs, the need to financially arrange, consolidation and oversee appropriated data innovation assets has surfaced.

Cloud sourcing joins conventional redistributing with the advantages of the cloud. Instead of just running your IT framework and applications for you, Cloud sourcing includes effectively moving both to the cloud. By maintaining your business on cloud-based IT applications and administrations, Cloud sourcing drastically brings down your IT costs and gives you the individuals and aptitude to make a virtual suite of SaaS applications that give a superior coordinated, progressively adaptable and flexible innovation establishment for your business activities. The combination of the two patterns - development of utilizations and stages to the cloud and re-appropriating of IT will drive this new Cloud sourcing IT model. By and by, financial matters, business needs and innovation advances will disturb current standards. In its least difficult state, cloud sourcing is made out of three fundamental components:

- Migration of on-premise application portfolios and foundation to cloud based, multi-tenant frameworks, stages and applications.
- Managed administrations to change and oversee support in this cloud condition including help-desk support, cloud activities, portfolio the executives, application advancement, testing upkeep and ceaseless improvement.
- A durable business and specialized interface to the cloud that edited compositions away the intricacy of dealing with different SaaS applications and cloud stages.

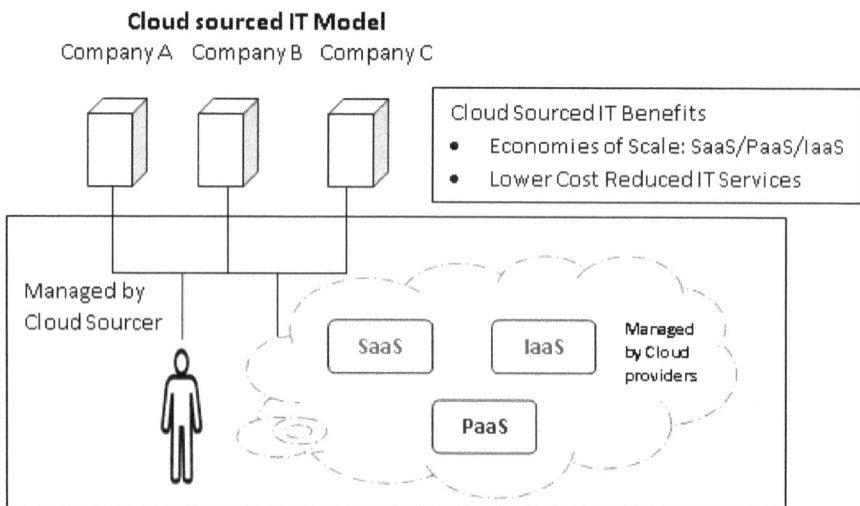

Figure 6. Cloud sourcing.

The client pays a clear expense dependent on qualities like income and salary of workers, and the Cloud source utilizes a mix of cloud applications/stages and their own administrations/IP to digest away a great part of the run of the mill multifaceted nature of big business IT. The Cloud source can focus on these considerable investment funds with improved degrees of administration for two essential reasons:

- The basic cost favourable circumstances and adaptability of cloud-based applications and administrations.
- A predetermined and reintegrated virtual cloud suite.

By taking a known blend of driving SaaS, PaaS, and IaaS suppliers, the cloud sourcing can give an incorporated arrangement of business capacities and innovation. Cloud sourcing on a very basic level adjusts the IT administrations model. By fundamentally lessening or notwithstanding wiping out zones of work regularly enveloped by redistributing contracts, cloud sourcing can concentrate on more value-added administrations for their clients, for example,

- Cloud checking - give tasks the board and oversight over an assorted arrangement of cloud advances and frameworks.
- Business model prototyping - utilizing cloud innovations to quickly model and demonstrate new business necessities and business forms.
- Platform application improvement - quickly creating and broadening applications utilizing cloud stages.
- Cloud reconciliation - integrating applications rapidly because of moving business forms.
- Legacy combination - interfacing with inheritance frameworks to give access to information by means of browser-based applications any place it's required.
- Mobility techniques - utilizing the cloud to empower simple versatile access.

Cloud sourcing do hold some customary inward and redistributed IT assignments including help work area, venture engineering, portfolio the board, and preparing/change the executives. From an IT and business point of view, Cloud sourcing offers an option in contrast to the decision between giving up control of a business procedure for cost reserve funds (Outsourced IT Model) or managing the significant expenses and unpredictability of supporting a whole foundation (Internal IT Model). Cloud stages give organizations an approach to control the pieces of the stack that issues most, the application and business procedure layer, and dynamic away the administration of framework. This methodology permits the IT group to concentrate their energies on driving advancement and supporting the business

Service Models

Cloud administration models portray how cloud administrations are made accessible to customers. Most basic help models incorporate a mix of IaaS (framework as an assistance), PaaS (stage as a help), and SaaS (programming as a help). These administration models may have collaborations between one another and be associated for instance, PaaS is reliant on IaaS since application stages require physical framework.

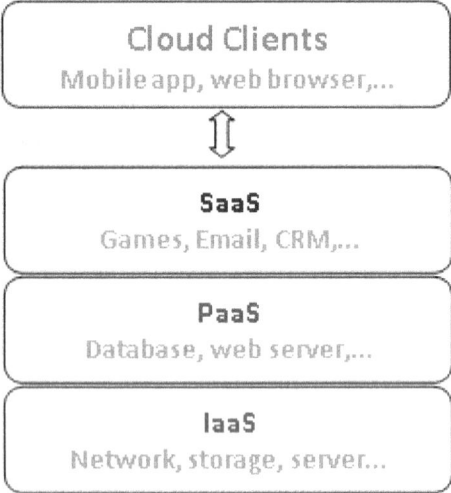

Figure 7. Cloud service model.

- The IaaS (Infrastructure as a Service) model gives foundation segments to customers. Segments may incorporate virtual machines, stockpiling, systems, firewalls, load balancers, etc. With IaaS, customers have direct access to the most minimal level programming in the stack - that is, to the working framework on virtual machines, or to the administration dashboard of a firewall or burden balancer. Amazon Web Services is one of biggest IaaS suppliers.

- The PaaS (Platform as a Service) model conveys a pre-assembled application stage to the customer; customers needn't invest energy building basic framework for their applications. On the backend, PaaS consequently scales, and arrangements required foundation segments relying upon application prerequisites. Regularly, PaaS arrangements give an API that incorporates a lot of capacities for automatic stage the board and arrangement advancement. Google AppEngine is a prevalent PaaS supplier, and Amazon Web Services additionally gives some PaaS arrangements notwithstanding IaaS contributions.
- SaaS (Software as a Service) gives prepared online programming arrangements. The SaaS programming supplier has full oversight of use programming. SaaS application models incorporate online mail; venture the board frameworks, CRMs, and internet-based life stages.

The primary distinction among SaaS and PaaS is that PaaS regularly speaks to a stage for application improvement, while SaaS gives online applications that are now created.

Infrastructure as a Service (IaaS)

Infrastructure as a Service (IaaS) is one of the three major help models of cloud computing close by PaaS and SaaS. Utilizing an Infrastructure as a Service (IaaS) will enable Customers to quickly include or evacuate limit, with charging against asset use. This gives a lot of adaptability and the capacity to hold expenses down. Similarly, as with all cloud computing administrations, it gives access to computing asset in a virtualized domain. It encourages quick sending of on-request benefits and the scaling of IT assets. The stage offers public sector bodies the capacity to share the expense of foundation between numerous associations, while exploiting most recent advancements, best practice arrangements and economies of scale. Physically, the pool of equipment asset is pulled from a huge number of servers and systems normally appropriated over various server farms, all of which the cloud supplier oversees keeping up. The customer, then again, is offered access to the virtualized segments to manufacture their own IT stages. In the same way as the other two types of cloud facilitating, IaaS can be used by big business customers to make financially savvy and effectively adaptable

IT arrangements where the complexities and costs of dealing with the hidden equipment are redistributed to the cloud supplier. On the off chance that the size of a business customer's activities varies, or they are hoping to grow, they can take advantage of the cloud asset as and when they need it as opposed to buy, introduce and incorporate equipment themselves.

IaaS clients are in charge of utilization advancement, organization and the executives. In an IaaS framework, virtual machines are by and large overcommitted to physical servers to expand benefit from equipment venture and chop down power spending plan. Cloud versatility in that condition tends to the test of asset provisioning for dynamic heap of virtual machines. For instance, if physical server can't fulfil the asset prerequisites of its virtual machines, some of them will be moved to different servers with the goal that application execution is guaranteed. A typical diagram of IAAS as shown below:

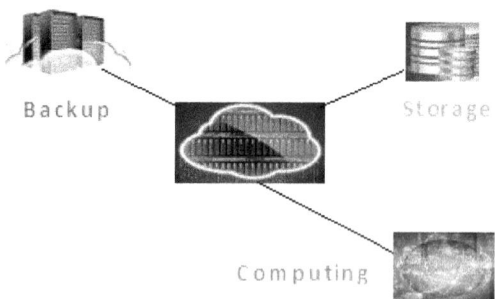

Figure 8. IaaS.

Advantages of IaaS

- IaaS is a viable model for outstanding tasks at hand that are brief, test or that change out of the blue. For instance, if a business is building up another product item, it may be more financially savvy to host and test the application utilizing an IaaS supplier. When the new programming is tried and refined, the business can expel it from the IaaS condition for a progressively conventional, in-house arrangement. On the other hand, the business could submit that bit of programming to a long haul IaaS arrangement, where the expenses of a long haul duty might be less.

- **Virtual data centers (VDC)**: A virtualized system of inter-connected virtual servers, which can be utilized to offer up-graded cloud facilitating abilities, endeavour IT foundation or to coordinate these tasks inside either an open or private cloud execution.
- **Faster**: Organizations pick IaaS since it is regularly simpler, quicker and more cost-productive to work an outstanding task at hand without purchasing, oversee and bolster the fundamental foundation. With IaaS, a business can basically lease or rent that foundation from another business.
- **Adaptability**: Asset is accessible as and when the customer needs it and there are no postponements in extending limit or the wastage of unused limit.
- **No interest in equipment**: The basic physical equipment that supports an IaaS administration is arrangement and kept up by the cloud supplier sparing the time and cost of doing as such on the customer side.
- **Utility style costing**: The administration can be got to on interest and customer pays for the asset that they really use.
- **Location independence**: The administration can more often than not be got to from any area so far as there is a web association and the security convention of the cloud permits it.
- **Pay as you go model**: All in all, IaaS clients pay on for each utilization premise, normally constantly, week or month. A few IaaS suppliers likewise charge clients dependent on the measure of virtual machine space they use.
- **Secured data centre locations**: Administrations accessible through an open cloud or private clouds facilitated remotely with the cloud supplier, advantage from the physical security stood to the servers, which are facilitated inside a server farm.
- **No single point failure**: On the off chance that one server or system switches, for instance, were to fall flat, the more extensive assistance would be unaffected because of the rest of the large number of equipment assets and excess arrangements.

Disadvantages of IaaS

- The information security issues due to multitenant engineering.

35

- Understanding is another normal issue for IaaS clients. Since IaaS suppliers claim the foundation, the subtleties of their framework arrangement and execution are once in a while straightforward to IaaS clients. This absence of straightforwardness can make frameworks the executives and checking progressively hard for clients.
- Merchant blackouts make clients unfit to get to their information for some time.
- Despite its flexible, pay-as-you-go model, IaaS billing can be a problem for some businesses. Cloud billing is extremely granular, and it is broken out to reflect the precise usage of services. It is common for users to experience sticker shock or finding costs to be higher than expected when reviewing the bills for every resource and service involved in an application deployment. Users should monitor their IaaS environments and bills closely to understand how IaaS is being used, and to avoid being charged for unauthorized services.
- The requirement for group preparing to figure out how to oversee new framework.

Platform as a Service (PaaS)

PaaS is basically worried about creating, sending and working client applications different capacities might be included, for example, the utilization of handling, stockpiling and system assets, however they are not the principle center. Customary on-premises for the situation of sending and working applications in a conventional on-premises condition, the client is liable for getting, introducing, designing and working every one of the components of the biological system required to run the applications. This incorporates all the equipment parts-servers, information stockpiling, and systems. It likewise regularly incorporates a broad programming stack, beginning with the working frameworks and different kinds of middleware and runtimes lastly the custom code of the applications themselves. There is likewise commonly a large group of supporting programming, including databases, informing frameworks, investigation programs, in addition to a broad arrangement of instruments for the executives and observing of the application underway. Also, programming is required for the arrangement and refreshing of the application programming

Platform-as-a-Service contributions essentially give a domain wherein to create, send and work applications. PaaS contributions normally include different application programming foundation abilities including application stages, reconciliation stages, business examination stages, occasion gushing administrations and portable back-end administrations. Furthermore, a PaaS offering regularly incorporates a lot of observing, the board, sending and related capacities. PaaS contributions are focused on fundamentally at application engineers, despite the fact that PaaS contributions additionally normally contain capacities that are important to administrators. PaaS in cloud processing is a system for programming creation conveyed over the web. This is the offering of a stage with inherent programming parts and apparatus, utilizing which designers can make, alter, test and dispatch applications. PaaS merchants oversee servers, working framework refreshes, security patches and reinforcements.

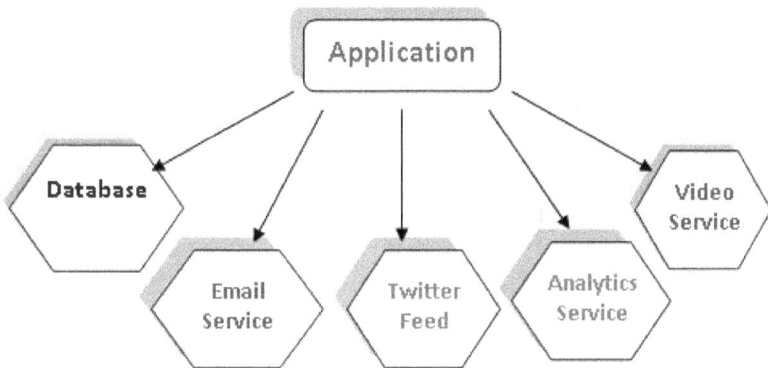

Figure 9. PaaS.

Advantages of PaaS

- Decreased costs for making, testing and propelling applications.
- Self-administration with diminished organization costs.
- The advancement procedure is enlivened and rearranged.
- Computerized organization arrangement.
- Decreased measure of coding required.
- Takes into consideration simple moving to the mixture cloud.

- PaaS-manufactured programming is profoundly adaptable, accessible and multi-tenant, as it is cloud-based.
- Support of group coordinated effort.
- Ability to include new clients rapidly.
- The help for automation gives both efficiency enhancements and furthermore consistency of conveyance.

Disadvantages of PaaS

- **Data security issues:** Sometime the information is cumbersome to such an extent that the creation procedure happens live on the remote server. This builds the archive's danger of being captured by other people who are fundamental outsiders to its origin.
- Compatibility of existing infrastructure.
- Dependency on vendor's speed, reliability and support.
- Information processing.
- Information interactivity.

Software as a Service (SaaS)

SaaS is a fresh out of the box new selling procedure for big business programming designers. SaaS is rising as a feasible re-appropriating alternative for customers keen on paying for the privilege to get to an institutionalized arrangement of business programming capacities through the system. SaaS model to a great extent supplanted the Application Service Providers (ASP) model, by making a design that gives no systems to altering the product on the seller side; all customization is done on the customer side through institutionalized interfaces. The way that sellers are not making any customer explicit ventures makes this redistributing model very fascinating. A few specialists explored customer's side determinants and the SaaS model reception, and drew on financial, key administration and Information Systems hypotheses to build up a hypothetical structure. By coordinating differing writing streams, they had the option to build up a progressively intricate perspective on vulnerability contending that a few sorts vulnerability increment the inclination to embrace SaaS, while different sorts don't. With the SaaS model, programming applications are sent on sellers' premises before a customer's appropriation. Customers don't buy programming or foundation (e.g., equipment and OS) forthright; however pay for their entrance to the administrations after some time. Usage cycle is abbreviated, since applications are as of now sent on SaaS merchants' destinations. The SaaS model additionally permits broad cost investment funds in working standard business segments on an enormous scale. As needs be, firms with significant expense of capital may discover the SaaS model progressively helpful as it empowers them to streamline on fixed capital expense by spreading the administration cost after some time, enables quicker time to esteem, and conceivably brings huge cost reserve funds The SaaS model is ending up progressively famous.

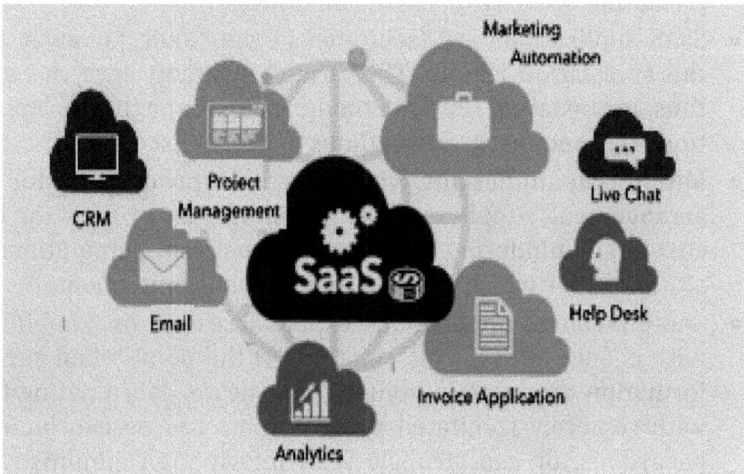

Figure 10. SaaS.

Advantages of SaaS

- SaaS empowers associations to make their product applications keep running in a virtual domain.
- SaaS in cloud figuring deals with this make organizations feasible enough to work in a virtual, adaptable yet dependable cloud condition.
- With SaaS, the enormous in advance capital cost gets decreased to a colossal rate.
- SaaS depends on an on-request administration, along these lines; associations can benefit its administrations according to their necessity to fit the staffing needs.

- SaaS arrangements are online; organization is speedy, fast and very simple.
- SaaS platform is effectively open as one can share and access any sort of data or information identified with the product application anytime of great importance from anyplace on the planet.

Disadvantages of SaaS

- Since information is being put away on the seller's servers, information security turns into an issue.
- SaaS applications are facilitated in the cloud, far away from the application clients. This brings inactivity into the earth; thus, for instance, the SaaS model isn't reasonable for applications that request reaction times in the milliseconds.
- Multi-occupant designs, which drive cost productivity for SaaS arrangement suppliers, limit customization of uses for huge customers, hindering such applications from being utilized in situations for which such customization is fundamental.
- Some business applications expect access to or combination with client's present information. At the point when such information are huge in volume or delicate, coordinating them with remotely facilitated programming can be exorbitant or hazardous, or can struggle with information administration guidelines.
- Organizations that embrace SaaS may discover they are constrained into receiving new forms, which may bring about unanticipated preparing costs or an expansion in likelihood that a client may make a blunder.

Deployment Models

A cloud deployment model is characterized by where the foundation for the organization lives and who has authority over that framework. Choosing which deployment model, you will go with is one of the most significant cloud sending choices you will make. Each cloud deployment model fulfils diverse hierarchical needs, so it's significant that you pick a model that will fulfil the necessities of your association. Maybe much progressively significant is the way that each cloud arrangement model has an alternate offer and various expenses related with it. In this manner, by and large, your decision of a cloud arrangement model may just come down to cash. Regardless, to have the option to settle on an educated choice, you should know about the attributes of every condition. The following are the cloud deployment models:

- Public Cloud
- Private Cloud
- Hybrid Cloud
- Community Cloud

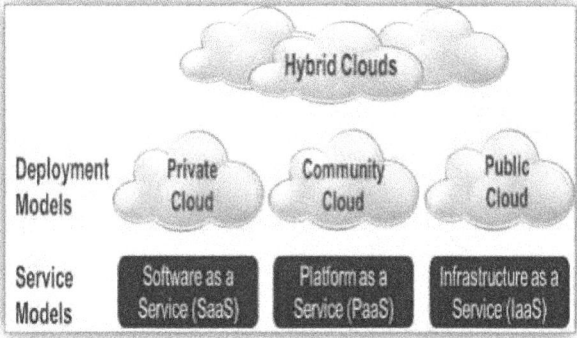

Figure 11. Deployment models.

Public Cloud

The cloud infrastructure is made available to the general public or a large industry group and is owned by an organization selling cloud services. In public clouds, resources are offered as a service, usually over an internet connection, for a pay-per-usage fee. Users can scale their own on demand and do not need to purchase hardware to use the service. Public cloud providers manage the infrastructure and pool resources into the capacity required by its users. A Public cloud is hosted on the internet and designed to be used by any user with an internet connection to provider a similar range of capabilities and services. Data created and submitted by consumers are usually stored on the servers of the third-party vendor. A public cloud is one base on the typical standard model, in which specialist organization makes assets, for example, stockpiling and application, reachable to the overall population over the Internet or through web applications/web administrations. Perhaps public cloud administrations are free or offered on a pay-as-you-go model. In public cloud equipment, application and data transfer capacity expenses are secured by the specialist organization so it is simple and reasonable set-up to the client. Examples of public cloud include:

- Amazon AWS
- Google Apps
- Salesforce.com
- Microsoft BPOS
- Microsoft Office 365

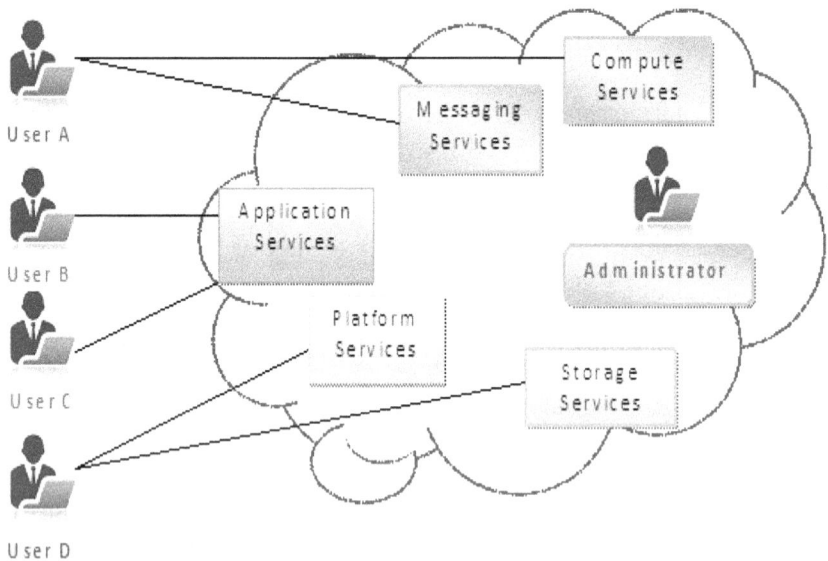

Figure 12. Public cloud.

Advantages of Public Cloud

- **Cost effective**: Since open cloud imparts same assets to enormous number of clients things being what they are, economical.
- **Dependability**: The open cloud utilizes huge number of assets from various areas. In the event that any of the assets comes up short, open cloud can utilize another.

- **Adaptability**: The open cloud can easily incorporate with private cloud, which gives clients an adaptable methodology.
- **Location independence**: Open cloud administrations are conveyed through internet, guaranteeing area freedom.
- **Utility style costing**: Open cloud is additionally founded on compensation per-utilize model and assets are available at whatever point client needs them.
- **High scalability**: Cloud assets are made accessible on interest from a pool of assets, i.e., they can be scaled up or down agreeing the prerequisite.

Disadvantages of Public Cloud

- **Low security**: In open cloud model, information is facilitated off-site and assets are shared freely, hence doesn't guarantee more significant level of security.
- **Less customizable**: It is relatively less adaptable than private cloud.

Private Cloud

A private cloud is likewise called as an inner cloud or corporate cloud, dwells inside the organization condition. The private cloud is a cloud foundation worked exclusively for a solitary association, regardless of whether oversaw inside or by an outsider and facilitated either inside or remotely. The cloud framework is gotten to just by the individuals from the association or potentially by allowed outsiders. The reason for existing isn't to offer cloud administrations to the overall population, yet to utilize it inside the association. A private cloud is facilitated in the server farm of an organization and suppliers its benefits just to clients inside that organization or its accomplices. A private cloud supplier more security than open clouds, and cost sparing depends on use of server farm. In the course of the most recent quite a long while, significant cloud administrations breaks have overwhelmed the features. Enterprises are paying heed and some are choosing that the private cloud less dangerous. Private cloud's capacity to virtualized administrations expands equipment use, at last decreasing expenses and multifaceted nature.

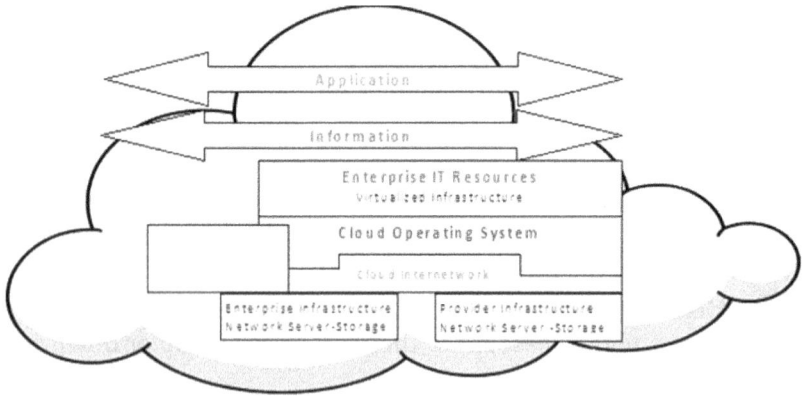

Figure 13. Private cloud.

Advantages of Private Cloud

- **High security and privacy**: Private cloud tasks are not accessible to overall population and assets are shared from particular pool of assets. In this way, it guarantees high security and protection.
- **More control**: The private cloud has more control on its assets and equipment than open cloud since it is gotten to just inside an association.
- **Cost and energy efficiency**: The private cloud assets are not as financially savvy as assets in open clouds however they offer more productivity than open cloud assets.

Disadvantages of Private Cloud

- **Limited area of operation**: The private cloud is just open locally and is extremely hard to convey internationally.
- **Costly**: Acquiring new equipment so as to satisfy the interest is an expensive exchange.
- **Constrained scalability**: The private cloud can be scaled distinctly inside limit of interior facilitated assets.
- **Extra skills**: So as to keep up cloud arrangement, association requires gifted mastery

Hybrid Cloud

A hybrid cloud condition is the blend of public and private cloud where the framework mostly facilitated inside the association and remotely in a public cloud. For instance, an association may utilize Amazon Simple Storage Service (Amazon S3) as public cloud administration to records their information and yet proceed in-house stockpiling for moment get to operational client information. Hybrid stockpiling clouds are frequently significant for record keeping and reinforcement work. It is a decent approach for a business to exploit the cost viability and adaptability.

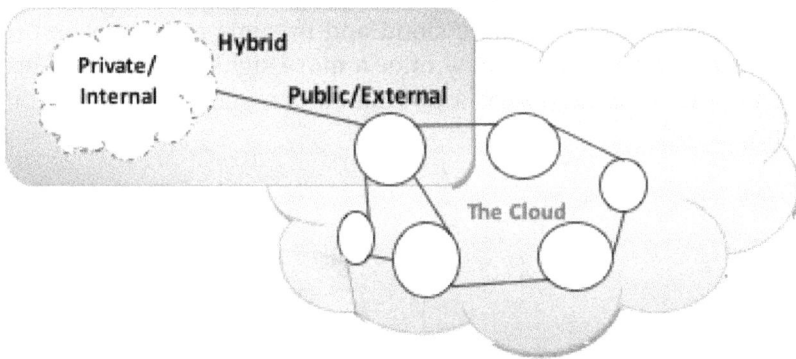

Figure 14. Hybrid cloud.

Advantages of Hybrid Cloud

- **Scalability**: It offers highlights of both, the public cloud versatility and the private cloud adaptability.
- **Adaptability**: It offers secure assets and versatile open assets.
- **Cost efficiency**: public clouds are more financially savvy than private ones. In this way, hybrid clouds can be cost sparing.
- **Security**: The private cloud in hybrid cloud guarantees higher level of security.

Disadvantages of Hybrid Cloud

- **Networking issues**: Networking winds up complex because of quality of private and open cloud.

- **Security compliance**: It is important to guarantee that cloud administrations are agreeable with security arrangements of the association.
- **Infrastructure dependency**: The hybrid cloud model is subject to inward IT framework; in this manner, it is important to guarantee laying-off across data centres.

Community Cloud

A community cloud can be perceived where various associations have equivalent necessities and exceptionally ready to share foundation in order to take in the advantages of cloud processing. Here costs augments than a public cloud and in some cases can be progressively costly however may offer a more significant level of protection and security. Google's Gov Cloud is a genuine case of community cloud.

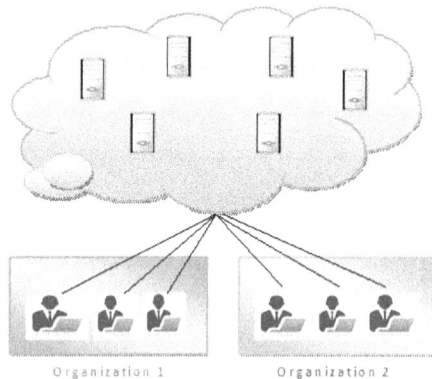

Figure 15. Community cloud.

Advantages of Community Cloud

- Cost of setting up a communal cloud versus singular private cloud can be less expensive because of the division of expenses among all members.
- Management of the community cloud can be redistributed to a cloud supplier. The favourable position here is that the supplier would be an unbiased outsider that is bound by agreement and that has no inclination to any of the customers inclu-

ded other than what is authoritatively ordered.

- Tools dwelling in the community cloud can be utilized to use the data put away to serve shoppers and the inventory network, for example, return following and in the nick of time generation and dispersion.

Disadvantages of Community Cloud

- Since all information is situated at one spot, one must be cautious in putting away information in network cloud since it may be open to other people.
- Costs higher than open cloud.
- It is challenging to distribute duties of administration, security and cost among associations.
- Fixed measure of transmission capacity and information stockpiling is shared among all network individuals.

Summary

Cloud computing architecture can be understood with the components and subcomponents of cloud such as storage, service, platform and infrastructure. Further, the three basic service models are discussed IaaS, PaaS and SaaS. This chapter also helps in understanding the cloud deployment according to the requirements of the clients.

References

1. Zhang Q, Cheng L, Boutaba R, Cloud Computing: state-of-the-art and research challenges, Journal of Internet Services and Applications, Volume 1, Pages 7-18, 2010, DOI: 10.1007/s13174-010-0007-6.
2. Cloud Service and Deployment Models: IEEE http://cloudcomputing.ieee.org/images/files/education/stud ygroup/Cloud_Service_and_DeploymentModels.pdf.
3. [Available online] https://en.wikipedia.org/wiki/Main_Page

Further Readings

1. Imran Ashraf, An overview of Service models of Cloud Computing, http://ijmcr.com/wp-content/uploads/2014/08/Paper18779-783.pdf

2. Diaby, Tinankoria, Bashari Rad, Babak, Cloud Computing: A review of the Concepts and Deployment Models, International Journal of Information Technology and Computer Science, Volume 9, Pages 50-58, 2017, DOI: 10.5815/ijitcs.2017.06.07.

3

Cloud Computing Services

Learning Objectives

- To understand the features, advantages and disadvantages of basic cloud services.
- Exploring the basic necessities of IaaS, PaaS and SaaS.
- To learn the importance of virtualization in Infrastructure as a service.
- To learn platform as a service can be useful in terms of business
- Exploring the applications related to these services.

Infrastructure as a Service (IaaS)

Infrastructure as an assistance urges organizations to move their physical infrastructure to the cloud with a level of control like what they would have in a customary on-premise data center. As opposed to acquiring or renting space in an exorbitant data center, work, land, and the entirety of the utilities to keep up and pass on PC servers, cloud frameworks and capacity, Cloud buyers rent space in a virtual information center from an IaaS provider. They approach the virtual information center by means of the Internet. Center data infrastructure sections are capacity, servers (figuring units), the framework itself, and the executives mechanical assemblies for infrastructure upkeep and checking. When renting from a cloud IaaS provider, customers are renting the equipment and the provisioning programming that computerizes it. While some little organizations have practical experience in just one of these IaaS cloud specialties, enormous cloud suppliers like Amazon or RightScale have contributions over all IaaS regions. In fact, the IaaS market has a generally low hindrance of section, yet it might require considerable money related interest so as to construct and bolster the cloud infrastructure. Develop open-source cloud the executives' structures like OpenStack are accessible to everybody, and give solid a product establishment to organizations that need to construct their private cloud or become an open cloud supplier. Hewlett-Packard as of late declared designs to offer open cloud administrations, and plan to manufacture their cloud utilizing OpenStack. A few other cloud suppliers, including Rackspace, have been running their administrations on OpenStack for a sometime.

Introduction to Virtualization

Virtualization normally alludes to the formation of virtual machine that can virtualize the entirety of the equipment assets, including processors, memory, storage, and system network. With the virtualization, physical equipment assets can be shared by at least one virtual machine. As indicated by the prerequisites from Popek and Goldberg, there are three perspectives to fulfil the virtualization. In the first place, the virtualization ought to give an equal domain to run a program contrasted with a local framework. In the event that the program shows an alternate conduct under the virtualization, it may not be qualified as a virtualized situation. The virtualization additionally needs to give a verified control of virtualized assets. Having a full control of assets is essential to ensure information and assets on each virtual condition from any dangers or execution obstruction in sharing physical assets. Virtualization regularly expects execution debasement because of the extra assignments for virtualization, however great execution ought to be accomplished with a product or equipment support in taking care of special directions. With these necessities, effective virtualization is ensured. In the accompanying segment, various kinds of hypervisors are clarified with the execution level of virtualization. Virtualized asset is additionally exhibited in CPU, memory and I/O exchanges.

The supporting for most of high-performing mists is a virtualized framework. Virtualization has been in server farms for quite a long while as a fruitful IT methodology for uniting servers. Utilized all the more comprehensively to pool foundation assets, virtualization can likewise give the essential building squares to your cloud condition to improve spryness and adaptability. Today, the essential concentration for virtualization keeps on being on servers. In any case, virtualizing capacity and systems is rising as a general technique.

Different Approaches to Virtualization

Virtualization is the utilization of programming and equipment to make the recognition that at least one elements exist despite the fact that the elements in really, are not physically present. Utilizing virtualization we can take one server seem, by all accounts, to be numerous, work station have all the earmarks of being running different working framework at the same time or a huge measure of plate space or drives to be accessible. The most widely recognized types of virtualization incorporate server virtualization, work area virtualization, virtual systems, and virtual storage. A hypervisor or virtual machine screen (VMM) is PC programming that makes and runs virtual machines. A hypervisor runs at least one virtual machines on a machine which is called as host machine. This machine can be a PC just as a server. Every one of the virtual machine is known as a visitor machine. The visitor working frameworks are spoken to by the hypervisor with a virtual working platform. It deals with the execution of the visitor working frameworks. There are different kinds of virtualizations are talked about beneath.

- **Server virtualization**: Making one server show up the same number of virtual server may run the equivalent or diverse working frameworks. So as to diminish the server inert time a solitary physical server is virtualized to shape various virtual servers. It very well may be inferred that the CPU use is the primary purpose behind server virtualization.
- **Work area virtualization**: This permits to switch between different working on the equivalent working frameworks, which makes the assignment simpler for programming designers and other analyzer staffs. This decreases the requirement for copy equipment and has other affordable viewpoints.
- **Virtual systems**: These make a deception that a client is associated legitimately to an organization system and assets, albeit no physical association may exist. Virtual systems are some of the time called VPN using a virtual private system the clients can interface with a system and access the assets from any web associated arrange.

Hypervisor

To get virtualization, hypervisor ought to be tended to first. Hypervisor empowers correspondence among equipment and a virtual machine so the virtualization achieves with this reflection layer (hypervisor). Hypervisor is initially called virtual machine screen (VMM) from. These two terms (Hypervisor and VMM) are commonly treated as equivalent words, however as indicated by the differ-entiation, a virtual machine screen (VMM) is a product that oversees CPU, memory, I/O information move, interfere, and the guidance set on a given virtualized condition. A hypervisor may allude to a work-ing framework (OS) with the VMM. There is a slight qualification among hypervisor and VMM however in this paper, we think about these terms to have indistinguishable implications to speak to a product for virtual machine. Ordinarily, a hypervisor can be parti-tioned into Type 1 and Type 2 hypervisor dependent on the distinc-tive degree of usage. Type 1 is perched on equipment and the corre-spondence among equipment and virtual machine is immediate. The host working framework isn't required in Type 1 hypervisor since it runs straightforwardly on a physical machine. Because of this ex-planation, it is here and there called an 'uncovered metal hypervi-sor'. VMware vSphere/ESXi, Microsoft Windows Server 2012 Hyper-V, Citrix XenServer, Red Hat Enterprise Virtualization (RHEV) and open-source Kernel-based Virtual Machine (KVM) are recognized in this classification. Type 2 hypervisor is on the working framework to oversee virtual machine effectively with the help of equipment arrangement from working framework. The additional layer among equipment and virtual machine in the sort 2 hypervisor causes wastefulness contrasted with the sort 1 hypervisor. VirtualBox and VMware Workstation are in this class. The terms of Host or Guest machine (or space) are utilized in the hypervisor to portray various jobs. Host machine (space) contains a hypervisor to oversee virtual machines, and Guest machine (area) implies each virtual machine sitting on a facilitated machine in a safe and detached condition with its very own consistent space. With these isolated jobs, the hypervi-sor can offer asset limits to different virtual machines on the equiva-lent physical machine. At the end of the day, the hypervisor is a product layer that makes a virtual situation with virtualized CPU, memory and I/O (storage and system) gadgets by abstracting cease-lessly the fundamental physical equipment. Virtual machine (VM) normally alludes to an embodied element including the working framework and the applications running in it also.

Virtual Machine Image

A VM is characterized as A method for making a physical PC work as though it were at least two PCs where each non-physical or virtual-ized PC (machine) is furnished with a similar fundamental design as that of a conventional physical PC. Virtualization innovation in this way permits the establishment of a working framework on equipment that doesn't generally exist". An OS is facilitated by the VM, with the previous speaking to the virtualisation component which makes it feasible for a visitor OS to run on a host PC. A very convenient element of distributed computing, multi-occupancy can be characterized as a property of a framework where numerous clients, alleged occupants, straightforwardly share the framework's assets, for example, administrations, applications, databases, or equipment, with the point of bringing down costs, while as yet having the option to only arrange the framework to the requirements of the inhabitant. Multi-occupancy can be separated into two classifications: different occurrence and local multi-tenure. With respects numerous example occupancy, each inhabitant profits by the administrations of a committed application occurrence from a common OS, equipment and middleware server in a facilitated domain. In any case, in connection to local multi-tenure, one case of a program can give administration to a few occupants over various facilitating assets. When taking a gander at the Software as a Service (SaaS) model, unmistakably multi-tenure can be connected to four differed programming layers: the virtual layer, the application layer, the OS layer, and the middleware layer. With respects a multi-occupancy virtualised condition, each client is relegated a VM that plays host to a visitor OS. It is conceivable that VMs having a place with various clients will have indistinguishable genuine assets because of asset pooling. The reason for the VMM is to organize the VMs and makes it feasible for the various OS occurrences to work on the equivalent physical equipment. With respects the multi-occupancy virtualised condition, certain security components have come into center, for example, VM separation, which relates to ensuring that VMs that capacity on indistinguishable physical equipment are kept separated from each other. VMs might be (moved) to different genuine hosts – a move which frequently happens in light of support, load adjusting, and adaptation to non-critical failure. It is conceivable that a VM which has been moved might be penetrated by an assailant and redistributed to a tainted VMM or precarious server. On the off chance that fundamental, it is conceivable to move back VMs to a previous state. This office gives the client a lot of adaptability, yet in addition offers ascend to security concerns; this is on the grounds that, when it occurs, the outcome might be a VM being presented again to a helplessness that had recently been settled. Moreover, it is conceivable for a VM to escape from the control of the VVM. This sort of VM can enable an aggressor to get to extra VMs in similar equipment, or incapacitate the VMM by and large. Another issue, known as VM spread, comes about when various VMs are being facilitated by a framework, yet most of said VMs are filling no need. This circumstance can prompt a critical misuse of the assets found inside the host machine. Among the most widely recognized dangers to the security of the cloud is VM picture sharing, essentially in light of the fact that the picture speaks to the underlying state for new VM examples. Thinking about both classification and respectability is indispensable if the VM picture is to be verified; this is because of the way that, on the off chance that an aggressor can increase unapproved get to and is vindictive, at that point said assailant can erase, adjust, and change overseer passwords, or define noxious VM occasions. Another hazard which surely exists is resistance and running unlicensed programming.

Resource Virtualization

The rise of inventive advances has totally changed the IT scene. Virtualization as an innovation that gives the capacity to intelligently isolate the physical assets of a server and use them as various detached machines called Virtual Machines. The CPU becomes numerous virtual CPUs, and same turns out to be valid for RAMs and Hard Disks.

What are the Different Resources that can be Virtualized in Cloud Computing?

As referenced over, software makes virtualization conceivable. This software is known as a Hypervisor, otherwise called a virtualization administrator. It sits between the equipment and the working framework, and relegates the measure of access that the applications and working frameworks have with the processor and other equipment assets. Since you have comprehended what is virtualization, how about we see how virtualization functions by contemplating distinctive virtualization strategies in distributed computing:

Hardware/Server Virtualization

We should comprehend what is Hardware/Server virtualization in a distributed computing and see its sorts. It is the most widely recognized sort of virtualization and it gives favorable circumstances like ideal equipment usage and application uptime. The essential thought is to consolidate numerous little physical servers into one huge physical server, with the goal that the processor can be utilized all the more successfully. The working framework that is running on a physical server gets changed over into a well-characterized OS that runs on the virtual machine.

Hardware virtualization likewise knows as hardware helped virtualization or server virtualization runs on the idea that an individual autonomous fragment of equipment or a physical server, might be comprised of different littler equipment sections or servers, basically combining various physical servers into virtual servers that run on a solitary essential physical server. Every little server can have a virtual machine, yet the whole bunch of servers is treated as a solitary gadget by any procedure mentioning the equipment. The hardware asset assignment is finished by the hypervisor. The primary points of interest incorporate expanded handling power because of boosted equipment usage and application uptime. The hypervisor controls the processor, memory, and different segments by enabling distinctive OS to run on a similar machine without the requirement for a source code.

In the vast majority of the cases, servers that virtualize equipment have a place with outsider providers that screen and keep up their operational state. That is the reason this innovation decreases gear related uses, yet in addition improves and streamlines the arrangement, accessibility and execution of the different outstanding tasks at hand.

Types

- Full Virtualization - Guest programming doesn't require any alterations since the fundamental equipment is completely recreated.
- Emulation Virtualization - The virtual machine re-enacts the equipment and gets autonomous of it. The visitor working framework doesn't require any adjustments.
- Para Virtualization - The equipment isn't mimicked and the visitor programming run their very own separated spaces.

Storage Virtualization

To homogenize storehouse, upgrade uptime, balance the heap and improve efficiency, organizations cause their putting away apparatuses to work in a virtual way as a unit. They can virtualize their in-house circles, tapes and other media in two habits: in connection to squares and individual documents.

Virtualized block storage permit getting to different gadgets paying little respect to their area and structure, in view of the division of a legitimate storehouse from a physical one. In instances of a document-based procedure, storage gives access to records that are kept on various hosts, which evacuates conditions among information and their physical area. Subsequently, organizations deal with their storage in a productive way and can relocate records consistently.

In this kind of virtualization, various system storage assets are available as a solitary storage gadget for simpler and progressively proficient administration of these assets. It gives different favourable circumstances as pursues:

- Improved storage the executives in a heterogeneous IT condition
- Easy refreshes, better accessibility
- Reduced personal time
- Better storage usage
- Automated the executives

Types

- Block- It works before the file system exists. It replaces controllers and takes over at the disk level. In this multiple storage devices are consolidated into one.
- File- The server that uses the storage must have software installed on it in order to enable file-level usage.

Network Virtualization

In network virtualization, numerous sub-systems can be made on the equivalent physical system, which might possibly is approved to speak with one another. This empowers confinement of record development crosswise over systems and upgrades security, and permits better observing and distinguishing proof of information utilization which gives the system overseer's scale a chance to up the system suitably. It additionally expands unwavering quality as an interruption in one system doesn't influence different systems, and the determination is simpler.

It alludes to the administration and observing of a PC arrange as a solitary administrative element from a single programming-based executive's support. It is expected to permit arrange improvement of information move rates, versatility, unwavering quality, adaptability, and security. It likewise mechanizes many system managerial assignments. System virtualization is explicitly helpful for systems that experience an enormous, fast, and flighty traffic increment. The intended result of network virtualization provides improved network productivity and efficiency.

Types

- **Internal:** Provide system like usefulness to a single unit.
- **External:** Combination of various systems into a single one, or isolation of a single system into numerous ones

Amazon EC2

Amazon Elastic Compute Cloud (Amazon EC2) gives adaptable figuring limit in the Amazon Web Services (AWS) cloud. Utilizing Amazon EC2 dispenses with your need to put resources into equipment in advance, so you can create and send applications quicker. You can utilize Amazon EC2 to dispatch the same number of or as hardly any virtual servers as you need, arrange security and organizing, and oversee capacity. Amazon EC2 empowers you to scale up or down to deal with changes in necessities or spikes in notoriety, lessening your need to conjecture traffic.

EC2 Components

In AWS EC2, the clients must know about the EC2 parts, their operating system support, safety efforts/security, estimating structures, and so forth.

Operating System Support

Amazon EC2 underpins different OS in which we have to pay extra authorizing charges like: Red Hat Enterprise, SUSE Enterprise and Oracle Enterprise Linux, UNIX, Windows Server, and so on. These OS should be actualized related to Amazon Virtual Private Cloud (VPC).

Security

Clients have full oversight over the deceivability of their AWS account. In AWS EC2, the security frameworks permit make gatherings and spot running occasions into it according to the prerequisite. You can determine the gatherings with which different gatherings may convey, just as the gatherings with which IP subnets on the Internet may talk.

Valuing

AWS offers an assortment of valuing choices, contingent upon the sort of assets, kinds of utilizations and database. It enables the clients to design their assets and figure the charges in like manner.

Adaptation to Internal Failure

Amazon EC2 enables the clients to get to its assets to configuration flaw tolerant applications. EC2 likewise contains geographic locales and disengaged areas known as accessibility zones for adaptation to internal failure and soundness. It doesn't share the definite areas of territorial server farms for security reasons.

Highlights of Amazon EC2

- Virtual processing conditions, known as samples.
- Preconfigured layouts for your occurrences, known as Amazon Machine Images (AMIs) that bundle the bits your requirement for your server.
- Various setups of CPU, memory, storage, and systems administration limit with based on occasions, known as case types.
- Secure login data for your cases utilizing key sets.
- Storage volumes for transitory information that is erased when you stop or end your case, known as case store volumes.

- Persistent storage volumes for your information utilizing the Amazon Elastic Block Store known as the Amazon EBS volumes.
- Multiple physical areas for your assets, for example, cases and Amazon EBS volumes, known as locales and Availability Zones.
- A firewall that empowers you to determine the conventions, ports, and source IP runs that can arrive at your cases utilizing security bunches.
- Static IPv4 addresses for dynamic distributed computing, known as Elastic IP addresses.
- Metadata, known as labels, which can make and relegate to your Amazon EC2 assets.
- Virtual systems you can make that are intelligently detached from the remainder of the AWS cloud, and that you can alternatively associate with your very own system, known as virtual private mists (VPCs).

Eucalyptus

Eucalyptus is a paid and open-source PC programming for building Amazon Web Services (AWS) perfect private and hybrid cloud computing situations, initially created by the organization Eucalyptus Systems. Eucalyptus is an abbreviation for Elastic Utility Computing Architecture for Linking Your Programs to Useful Systems. Eucalyptus empowers pooling register, storage, and system assets that can be powerfully scaled up or down as application remaining burdens change.

Components of Eucalyptus

- **Cluster controller (CC)**: Cluster Controller deals with the at least one Node controller and answerable for sending and overseeing occurrences on them. It speaks with Node Controller and Cloud Controller at the same time. CC additionally deals with the systems administration for the running occurrences under particular kinds of systems administration modes accessible in Eucalyptus.
- **Cloud controller (CLC)**: Cloud Controller is front end for the whole biological system. CLC gives an Amazon EC2/S3 agreeable web administrations interface to the customer instru-

ments on one side and associates with the remainder of the parts of the Eucalyptus foundation on the opposite side.

- **Node controller (NC)**: It is the fundamental segment for Nodes. Hub controller keeps up the existence cycle of the occasions running on every hub. Hub Controller communicates with the OS, hypervisor and the Cluster Controller all the while.
- **Walrus storage controller (WS3)**: Walrus Storage Controller is a basic document storage framework. WS3 stores the machine pictures and depictions. It likewise stores and serves records utilizing S3 APIs.
- **Capacity controller (SC)**: Allows the creation of snapshots of volumes. It provides persistent block storage over AoE or SCSI to the instances.

Highlights

- Eucalyptus can run different adaptations of Windows and Linux virtual machine pictures. Clients can manufacture a library of Eucalyptus Machine Images (EMIs) with application metadata that are decoupled from framework subtleties to enable them to run on Eucalyptus mists. Amazon Machine Images are likewise perfect with Eucalyptus mists. VMware Images and Apps can be changed over to run on Eucalyptus mists and AWS open mists.
- Eucalyptus client personality the board can be incorporated with existing Microsoft Active Directory or LDAP frameworks to have fine-grained job based access command over cloud assets.
- Eucalyptus underpins capacity territory arrange gadgets to exploit storage exhibits to improve execution and unwavering quality. Eucalyptus Machine Images can be sponsored by EBS-like relentless storage volumes, improving the presentation of picture dispatch time and empowering completely diligent virtual machine examples. Eucalyptus additionally supports direct-joined storage
- Eucalyptus is an open source Linux based programming design which gives an EC2-good distributed computing platform and S3-perfect distributed storage platform. It actualizes adaptable, productive improving and private and cross breed mists inside and association's IT foundation. It gives an Infra-

structure as a Service (IaaS) arrangement. Clients can utilize product equipment.

Platform as a Service (PaaS)

PaaS in the context of cloud computing cloud computing is characterized as a worldview for empowering system access to an adaptable and flexible pool of sharable physical and virtual assets with self-administration provisioning and organization on request. The physical and virtual assets are offered as capacities by cloud administrations, conjured through a characterized interface. The assets incorporate servers, information stockpiling gadgets, systems, working frameworks, programming and applications. Cloud computing offers practically the entirety of the abilities of IT frameworks through cloud benefits that are summoned over the system and it is the sheer broadness of capacities that can be a test for the cloud administration client to get it.

Platform as-a-Service contributions essentially give a situation wherein to create, send and work applications. PaaS contributions regularly include different application programming foundation (middleware) abilities including application platforms, reconciliation platforms, business examination platforms, occasion spilling administrations and versatile back-end administrations. What's more, a PaaS offering frequently incorporates a lot of observing, the board, sending and related capacities. PaaS contributions are focused on basically at application engineers, despite the fact that PaaS contributions additionally ordinarily contain abilities that are important to administrators. One method for portraying PaaS is that it speaks to a cloud administration rendering of the application framework offered by substances, for example, application servers, database the executives frameworks, coordination agents, business process the board frameworks, rules motors and complex occasion handling frameworks. Such application framework helps the application designer recorded as hard copy business applications decreasing the measure of code that should be composed simultaneously as growing the useful abilities of the applications. The embodiment of a PaaS framework is that the cloud specialist organization assumes liability for the establishment, arrangement and activity of the application foundation, leaving just the application code itself to the cloud administration client. PaaS contributions additionally frequently develop the platform capacities of middleware by offering application engineers a differing and developing arrangement of administrations and APIs that give explicit usefulness in an oversaw, constantly accessible style. This methodology expects to cloud the way that there is middleware present by any stretch of the imagination, empowering prompt profitability for engineers. Also, PaaS contributions give their capacities in a way that empowers the applications to exploit the local qualities of cloud frameworks, frequently without the application designer adding extraordinary code to the application itself. This gives a course to building conceived on the cloud applications without requiring specific abilities. PaaS can be stood out from SaaS contributions: SaaS offers a fixed arrangement of use abilities while PaaS bolsters the creation and utilization of use code with whatever arrangement of capacities is required for the business. The requirement for particular code is general and it is telling that numerous SaaS contributions give APIs explicitly to give to fitting, customization and expansion utilizing applications based on a PaaS. Thus, PaaS can be appeared differently in relation to IaaS contributions: IaaS gives basic framework however leaves establishment, setup and activity of the fundamental programming stacks in the hands of the cloud administration client. A PaaS offering gives the application middleware stacks prepared to-run and oversaw by the supplier. IaaS contributions give broad power over assets which might be essential for certain applications, yet at the expense of requiring significant exertion with respect to the cloud administration client. PaaS contributions frequently sort out the basic assets, expelling the duty and exertion from the cloud administration client yet conceivably restricting decisions. Some PaaS contributions additionally mix in highlights of IaaS and SaaS cloud administrations offering some control of essential asset allotment from one perspective and giving total off-the-rack programming capacities on the other. This can cause some disarray however the sign of a PaaS framework is the capacity for the cloud administration client to make and run applications and administrations that meet explicit business needs.

PaaS frameworks can be sent as open cloud administrations or as private cloud administrations. Private cloud organization might be less effective than open cloud arrangement, because of diminished open doors for asset sharing expanding costs. Private cloud arrangement may require the cloud administration client to have had some expertise in house abilities for introducing and working the PaaS framework something that can be left to the cloud specialist co-op for open cloud sending. On-premises arrangement puts the onus on the cloud administration client to actualize strength and reinforcement capacities that might be given out-of-the-crate by an open cloud organization.

Characteristics of Platform as a Service

- **Support for custom applications**: Backing for the improvement, arrangement and activity of custom applications. PaaS contributions ordinarily support conceived on the cloud or cloud local applications that can exploit the adaptable, versatile and appropriated abilities of cloud framework. As a rule, this is accomplished without the application designer composing extraordinary code to exploit these capacities.
- **Provision of runtime conditions**: Ordinarily each runtime condition bolsters, it is possible that one or a little arrangement of programming dialects and systems for instance Node.js, Ruby and PHP runtimes. A normal for some PaaS contributions is support for a scope of runtime situations, as opposed to only a couple rather than earlier non-cloud middleware stages. This empowers engineers to pick the most fitting innovation for the errand close by something that is getting progressively pervasive as bilingual conditions become increasingly acknowledged in the business.
- **Rapid sending components**: It is average of numerous PaaS contributions to furnish engineers and administrators with a push and run instrument for sending and running applications giving unique assignment of assets when the application code is passed to the PaaS by means of an API. Setup prerequisites are kept to a base of course, in spite of the fact that there is the ability to control the design whenever required for instance, controlling the quantity of parallel running examples of an application so as to deal with the foreseen remaining burden or to meet versatility objectives.
- **Support for a scope of middleware abilities**: Applications have an assortment of prerequisites and this is reflected in the arrangement of a wide scope of use foundation that supports a scope of abilities. One is database the board, with both SQL and NoSQL database advances gave. Different capacities in-

corporate mix administrations, business process the executives, business examination administrations, rules motors, occasion handling administrations and portable back-end administrations.

- **Provision of administrations**: Backing for the application designer for the most part comprises of something beyond middleware numerous capacities are given as a progression of discrete administrations, regularly summoned through an API or some likeness thereof.

- **Preconfigured capacities**: Numerous PaaS frameworks are described by abilities that are preconfigured by the supplier, with at least arrangement accessible to designers and client tasks staff. This decreases multifaceted nature, builds efficiency and brings down the potential for sudden issues, with capacities less difficult to oversee and simpler to investigate.

- **API Management abilities**: It is progressively the situation that business applications need to uncover a few abilities by means of APIs. Sometimes, this is required by the idea of the UI to the application portable applications for the most part need an API so that while working autonomously of the business application, they can get to information and exchanges when required. In different cases, some portion of the business arrangement is to empower different gatherings to coordinate their very own business applications with those of the venture this combination is done through an API. Giving an API requires a level of control, with the goal that lone approved clients can get to the API and every client can just get to those capacities for which they have authorization. Offering an API requires some measure of API Management.

- **Security abilities**: Security is one of the most significant parts of any business arrangement thus it isn't astonishing to find that PaaS contributions give worked in security abilities, lessening the heap on engineers and administrators to give and deal with these capacities. Capacities incorporate firewall, endpoint the executives, secure convention dealing with, access and approval, encryption of information moving and very still, respectability checking, and so on. PaaS frameworks can offer these capacities with insignificant or no effect on application code, streamlining the developer's assignments.

- **Tools to help engineers**: A point of numerous PaaS frameworks is to bind together and streamline advancement and tasks for frameworks as it were, support DevOps by separating the divisions among improvement and activities that have usually existed for in-house frameworks. PaaS frameworks help the application lifecycle by giving advancement apparatuses including code editors, code storehouses, manufacture instruments, sending devices, test devices and administrations and security devices. It is additionally basic to locate a lot of utilization observing and investigation administrations, including abilities, for example, logging, log examination and application use examination and dashboards.

- **Operations capacities**: PaaS frameworks help administrators through tasks capacities both for the applications and for the PaaS framework itself, by means of dashboards and regularly by means of APIs that empower clients to connect their very own activities toolsets. In this way, for instance, abilities to increment or diminishing the quantity of running cases of an application are normal now and again took care of via robotized administrations that change the quantity of occurrences dependent on a lot of rules set up by the client tasks staff.

What is Service Oriented Architecture (SOA)?

The Service Oriented Architecture is a compositional structure which incorporates accumulation of services in a system which speaks with one another. The obscurity of each service isn't observable to other help. The service is a sort of activity which is very much characterized, independent that gives separate usefulness, for example, checking client records, printing bank declarations and so forth and doesn't rely upon the slake of different services.

Importance of SOA

- SOA is broadly utilized in showcase which reacts rapidly and makes viable changes as per advertise circumstances.
- The SOA keep mystery the usage subtleties of the subsystems.
- It permits collaboration of new channels with clients, accomplices and providers.
- It approves the organizations to choose programming or equipment of their decision as it goes about as stage autonomy.

Features

- SOA utilizes interfaces which take care of the troublesome combination issues in enormous frameworks.
- SOA conveys clients, suppliers and providers with messages by utilizing the XML pattern.
- It utilizes the message observing to improve the presentation estimation and identifies the security assaults.
- As it reuses the administration, there will be lower programming improvement and the executive's costs.

Advantages

- **Component reuse**: SOA permits reusing the administration of a current framework and, on the other hand, fabricating the new framework.
- **Organizational agility**: It permits connecting new administrations or redesigning existing administrations to put the new business necessities.
- It can improve the exhibition, usefulness of a help and effectively makes the framework overhaul.
- SOA has capacity to alter or change the distinctive outer situations and the enormous applications can be overseen effectively.
- **Language-neutral integration**: The foundational contemporary web services standards use extensible Mark-up Language, which is focused on the creation and consumption of delimited text. Regardless of the development language used, these systems can offer and invoke services through a common mechanism. Programming language neutrality is a key differentiator from past integration approaches.
- **Leveraging existing systems**: One common use of SOA is to define elements or functions of existing application systems and make them available to the enterprise in a standard agreed-upon way, leveraging the substantial investment already made in existing applications

Disadvantages

- SOA requires high adventure cost.

- There is progressively noticeable overhead when an assistance interfaces with another help which grows the response time and machine load while endorsing the data parameters.
- SOA isn't proper for GUI (graphical UI) applications which will end up being continuously erratic when the SOA requires the staggering data exchange.

Cloud Platform and Management

A cloud management stage is an assortment of composed programming devices that an association can use to screen and control cloud preparing resources. While an affiliation can use a cloud the executives arrange just for a private or public cloud association, these toolsets regularly target cross breed and multi-cloud models to help join control of various cloud-based establishments. The precise rundown of abilities of a cloud the board arranges moves by shipper. Some offer a sweeping plan of contraptions, while others target more claim to fame adventures or vertical markets. Also, a couple of dealers pass on cloud the executives organize as on-premises applications, while others pass on them as programming as a help. Overall, cloud the board insinuates the movement of administrative order over open, private, half breed and multi-cloud courses of action.

Capabilities of a Cloud Management Platform

- **General administrations**: Provides client self-administration abilities, just as detailing and examination highlights to pick up understanding into cloud services
- **Service management**: Enables an IT group to screen cloud-based administrations to help with scope quantification, remaining burden organization and guaranteeing all accessibility and execution prerequisites are met;
- **Resource management**: Provides instruments to oversee cloud processing assets, for example, virtual machines, storage and systems, with capacities, for example, asset revelation, labelling, provisioning, computerization and coordination. What's more, the cloud management stage may incorporate abilities to relocate assets between situations, for example, private and open clouds.
- **Financial management**: Offers capacities to naturally follow

and allot cloud computing spend to explicit clients or business divisions. All in all, these budgetary management includes likewise incorporate the capacity to create chargeback reports and estimate future cloud costs.

- **Governance and security**: Allow an administrator to authorize approach-based control of cloud assets, and offers security highlights, for example, encryption and identity access management.

Examples

Google App Engine (GAE)

GAE is a Platform as a Service and cloud computing stage for creating and facilitating web applications in Google-oversaw server farms. Applications are sandboxed and stumbled into numerous servers. Application Engine offers programmed scaling for web applications as the quantity of solicitations increments for an application, App Engine consequently dispenses more assets for the web application to deal with the extra request.

Google App Engine is free up to a specific degree of expended assets and just in standard condition however not in adaptable condition. Expenses are charged for extra storage, data transfer capacity, or example hours required by the application.

Features

- App Engine gives more frameworks to make it simple to compose versatile applications, yet can just run a constrained scope of utilizations intended for that foundation.
- App Engine's framework evacuates a considerable lot of the framework organization and advancement difficulties of building applications to scale to many demands every second and beyond. Google handles sending code to a group, checking, failover, and propelling application occasions as important.
- App Engine allows designers to utilize just its supported languages, APIs, and structures. Current APIs permit putting away and recovering information from the record arranged Google Cloud Datastore database; making HTTP demands; sending email; controlling pictures; and storing. Google Cloud

SQL can be utilized for App Engine applications requiring a social MySQL good database backend.

- Per-day and per-minute quantities limit transfer speed and CPU use, number of solicitations served, number of simultaneous demands, and calls to the different APIs, and individual demands are ended on the off chance that they take over 60 seconds or return more than 32MB of information.

Microsoft Azure

Microsoft Azure is a cloud computing administration made by Microsoft for building, testing, conveying, and overseeing applications and administrations through Microsoft-oversaw server farms. It gives programming as a help (SaaS), stage as an assistance (PaaS) and foundation as a help (IaaS) and supports a wide range of programming dialects, instruments and structures, including both Microsoft-explicit and outsider programming and frameworks.

Azure was reported in October 2008, began with codename Venture Red Dog, and discharged on February 1, 2010, as Windows Azure before being renamed Microsoft Azure on March 25, 2014.

Features

- The by and large cost is low as the assets are assigned on request and servers are consequently refreshed.
- It is less vulnerable as servers are consequently refreshed and being checked for all realized security issues. The entire procedure isn't noticeable to designer and in this way doesn't represent a danger of information rupture.
- Since new forms of advancement apparatuses are tried by the Azure group, it turns out to be simple for engineers to proceed onward to new devices. This likewise encourages the engineers to satisfy the client's need by rapidly adjusting to new forms.

Salesforce.com

Salesforce.com Inc. is an American cloud-based programming organization headquartered in San Francisco, California. In spite of the fact that the heft of its income originates from its client relationship the board (CRM) administration, Salesforce likewise sells a reciprocal suite of big business applications concentrated on client support, showcasing mechanization, examination and application advancement.

Features

- Account and Contact Management
- Opportunity Management and Score
- Lead Management
- Sales Data
- File Sync
- File Sharing

Software as a Service (SaaS)

Software as a service is a cloud administrations conveyance model that offers an on-request online software membership. Similarly, as with other cloud conveyance models, SaaS offers organizations the chance to diminish inward IT bolster expenses and move support risk to the SaaS supplier. SaaS is by a long shot the most broadly utilized cloud conveyance model in light of the fact that pretty much every software seller is hoping to put its offering on the SaaS rails there are SaaS contributions in each class of software item. SaaS is the final product, enabling organizations to convey software on request to clients. With SaaS, sellers can give software through the web to clients and clients. An associated gadget and program are for the most part clients need to access and utilize the software.

Likewise alluded to as cloud application services, SaaS is the most prominent choice for B2B organizations in the distributed computing market as a result of its numerous advantages. With the software facilitated and running in the cloud, you don't have to experience any downloads and establishments. Set up and execution is simple and speedy. You'll be fully operational and utilizing the software in a matter of moments without its need understanding or IT specialists. The seller deals with all the specialized side security, stockpiling, servers, middleware and that's only the tip of the iceberg. Our last similarity travel as assistance compares SaaS to a comprehensive get-away where the basics booking, settlements, transport, nourishment, and so on are altogether dealt with.

Characteristics

- SaaS makes the software accessible over the Internet.
- The software applications are kept up by the merchant.
- The permit to the software might be membership based or utilization based. Also, it is charged on repeating premise.
- SaaS applications are financially savvy since they don't require any upkeep at end client side.
- They are accessible on request.
- They can be scaled up or down on request.
- They are consequently overhauled and refreshed.
- SaaS offers shared information model. Along these lines, numerous clients can share single example of framework. It isn't required to hard code the usefulness for singular clients.
- All clients run a similar form of the software.

Advantages

Using SaaS has proved to be beneficial in terms of scalability, efficiency and performance. Some of the benefits are listed below:

- **Modest software tools**
  The SaaS application sending requires an almost no customer side software establishment, which brings about the accompanying advantages:
  o No prerequisite for complex software bundles at customer side
  o Little or no danger of setup at customer side
  o Low dissemination cost
- **Efficient utilization of software licenses:** The client can have single permit for various PCs running at various areas which lessens the authorizing cost. Likewise, there is no prerequisite for permit servers on the grounds that the software runs in the supplier's foundation.
- **Centralized management and data:** The cloud supplier stores information midway. Be that as it may, the cloud suppliers may store information in a decentralized way for excess and dependability.
- Platform responsibilities managed by providers: All stage duties, for example, reinforcements, framework upkeep, securi-

ty, equipment revive, control the executives and so on are performed by the cloud supplier. The client doesn't have to make a big deal about them.

- **Multitenant solutions**: Multitenant arrangements enable various clients to share single case of various assets in virtual disconnection. Clients can tweak their application without influencing the center usefulness.

Disadvantages

- **Browser based risks**: If the client visits noxious site and program gets tainted, the ensuing access to SaaS application may bargain the client's information. To maintain a strategic distance from such dangers, the client can utilize various programs and devote a particular program to get to SaaS applications or can utilize virtual work area while getting to the SaaS applications.
- **Network dependence**: The SaaS application can be conveyed just when system is ceaselessly accessible. Likewise, system ought to be solid however the system unwavering quality can't be ensured either by cloud supplier or by the client.
- **Lack of portability between SaaS clouds**: Transferring outstanding tasks at hand starting with one SaaS cloud then onto the next isn't so natural since work process, business rationales, UIs, bolster contents can be supplier explicit.

Web Services

A web service is an assortment of open conventions and models utilized for trading information between applications or frameworks. Programming applications written in different programming dialects and running on different stages can utilize web services to trade information over PC systems like the Internet in a way like between process correspondences on a solitary PC. This interoperability is because of the utilization of open models.

Characteristics

- **XML-based**: Web services use XML at information portrayal and information transportation layers. Utilizing XML takes out any systems administration, working framework, or stage official. Web services-based applications are profoundly interoperable at their centre level.

- **Loosely coupled**: A shopper of a web service isn't attached to that web service straightforwardly. The web service interface can change after some time without trading off the customer's capacity to associate with the service. A firmly coupled framework suggests that the customer and server rationale are firmly attached to each other, inferring that in the event that one interface changes, the other must be refreshed. Receiving an approximately coupled design will in general make programming frameworks progressively sensible and permits easier combination between various frameworks.

- **Coarse-grained**: Object-oriented innovations, for example, Java uncover their services through singular strategies. An individual technique is too fine an activity to give any valuable capacity at a corporate level. Building a java program without any preparation requires the formation of a few fine-grained techniques that are then created into a coarse-grained service that is devoured by either a customer or another service. Organizations and the interfaces that they uncover ought to be coarse-grained. Web services innovation gives a characteristic method for characterizing coarse-grained services that entrance the perfect measure of business rationale.

- **Ability to be synchronous or asynchronous**: Synchronicity alludes to the authoritative of the customer to the execution of the service. In synchronous summons, the customer squares and trusts that the service will finish its activity before proceeding. Offbeat tasks enable a customer to conjure a service and afterward execute different capacities. Non-concurrent customers recover their outcome at a later point in time, while synchronous customers get their outcome when the service has finished. Offbeat ability is a key factor in empowering inexactly coupled frameworks.

- **Supports remote procedure call (RPC)**: Web services enable customers to summon methodology, capacities, and strategies on remote objects utilizing a XML-based convention. Remote systems uncover information and yield parameters that a web service must bolster. Segment improvement through Enterprise JavaBeans (EJBs) and .NET Components has progressively become a piece of structures and venture organizations over the recent years. The two innovations are dispersed and available through an assortment of RPC components. A web service underpins RPC by giving services of its own, comparable to those of a conventional segment, or by making an interpretation of approaching summons into a conjuring of an EJB or a .NET part.

Web 2.0

With regards to characterize web 2.0, the term means such web applications which enable sharing and cooperation chances to individuals and help them to communicate on the web. Web 2.0 is the business unrest in the PC business brought about by the transition to the web as a stage, and an endeavour to comprehend the principles for progress on that new stage.

It's an essentially improved form of the principal internet, portrayed explicitly by the change from static to dynamic or client produced content and furthermore the development of web-based social networking. The idea driving Web 2.0 alludes to rich web applications, web-situated design and social web. It alludes to changes in the manner's web pages are planned and utilized by the clients, with no adjustment in any specialized determinations.

Characteristics

- Static pages rather than dynamic HTML.
- Content gave from the server's file system rather than a social database the board framework (RDBMS).
- Pages assembled utilizing Server Side Includes or Common Gateway Interface (CGI) rather than a web application written in a unique programming language, for example, Perl, PHP, Python or Ruby.
- The utilization of HTML 3.2-time components, for example, casings and tables to position and adjust components on a page. These were frequently utilized in blend with spacer GIFs.
- Proprietary HTML expansions, for example, the <blink> and <marquee> labels, presented during the principal program war.
- Online guest books.

- GIF catches, designs (ordinarily 88x31 pixels in size) advancing web programs, working frameworks, word processors and different items.
- HTML structures sent by means of email. Backing for server side scripting was uncommon on shared servers during this period. To give an input instrument to web website guests, mailto structures were utilized. A client would fill in a structure, and after tapping the structures submit button, their email customer would dispatch and endeavour to send an email containing the structure's subtleties. The prevalence and difficulties of the mailto convention drove program engineers to fuse email customers into their programs.

Advantages

- Available whenever, wherever.
- Variety of media.
- Ease of use.
- Learners can effectively be engaged with information building.
- Can make dynamic learning networks.
- Everybody is the creator and the supervisor; each alter that has been made can be followed.
- User well disposed.
- Updates in wiki are quick and it offers more hotspots for scientists.
- Provides ongoing dialog.

Web OS

Web OS, otherwise called LG Web OS and recently known as Open Web OS, HP Web OS and Palm Web OS is a Linux part based performing multiple tasks working framework for savvy gadgets, for example, shrewd TVs and it has been utilized as a portable working framework. At first created by Palm, Inc. (which was procured by Hewlett-Packard), HP made the stage open source, so, all in all it became Open Web OS. The working framework was later offered to LG Electronics. In January 2014, Qualcomm reported that it had obtained innovation licenses from HP, which incorporated all the Web OS and Palm licenses.

Different forms of Web OS have been highlighted on a few gadgets since propelling in 2009, including Pre, Pixi, and Veer cell phones, TouchPad tablet, LG's brilliant TVs since 2014, LG's shrewd iceboxes and keen projectors since 2017.

Characteristics

- **Multitasking interface**: Navigation utilizes multi-contact gestures on the touch screen. The interface utilizes cards to oversee performing multiple tasks and speak to applications. The client switches between running applications with a flick from left and right on the screen. Applications are shut by flicking a card up and off the screen. The application cards can be improved for association. Web OS 2.0 presented stacks, where related cards could be stacked together.
- **Synergy**: Palm alluded to joining of data from numerous sources as Collaboration. Users can sign into various email accounts from various suppliers and coordinate these sources into a solitary list. Comparative abilities pull together schedules and furthermore texts and SMS instant messages from various sources.
- **Over-the-air updates**: The OS can be refreshed without docking to a PC, rather accepting OS refreshes over the transporter association.
- **Sync**: By default, information adjusts utilizes a cloud-based approach as opposed to utilizing a work area match up customer. The principal form of web OS transported with the capacity to synchronize with Apple's iTunes programming by taking on the appearance of an Apple gadget, however this component was incapacitated by ensuing iTunes programming refreshes.

Summary

The basic service models of cloud are IaaS, PaaS and SaaS. These models eliminate the need of hardware, application and storage which makes up the architecture of cloud. For any small-scale business organizations cloud services can be useful on basis of economy. More about the services can be understood through the examples provided.

References

1. NIST   Definition   of   Cloud   Computing,
   https://www.nist.gov/programsprojects/cloud-computing.
2. Rajkumar Buyya, Karthik Sukumar, Platforms for Building and
   Deploying Applications for Cloud Computing, April 2011.
3. [Available   online]
   https://en.wikipedia.org/wiki/Cloud_computing

Further Readings

1. Cloud Service Models - javatpoint
2. What is Cloud Services? | Cloud Services Definition (webope-
   dia.com)
3. Infrastructure as a service - Wikipedia
4. Platform as a service - Wikipedia
5. Software as a service - Wikipedia

4

Cloud Operating System

Learning Objectives

- Understanding CloudOS
- To learn the requirements of CloudOS
- To understand CloudOS architecture
- Giving an insight on goals and benefits of CloudOS
- Get to know about different types of CloudOS

Like a server Operating System (OS), a cloud OS is liable for overseeing assets. In a server (e.g., a PC), the OS is liable for dealing with the different equipment assets, for example, CPU, memory, plates, arrange interfaces everything inside a server's body. A cloud operating system is another sort of programming that is intended to have numerous kinds of programming that are executed over a gathering of equipment dispersed over the cloud. It shrouds the equipment activity subtleties and enables these rare assets to be effectively shared. A cloud OS fills a similar need. Rather than dealing with a solitary machine's assets, a cloud OS is answerable for dealing with the cloud framework, stowing away the cloud framework subtleties from the application software engineers and organizing the sharing of the restricted assets. Be that as it may, in contrast to a conventional OS, a cloud OS needs to do everything at scale. For instance, it is accounted for that Google has well more than 1 million servers. Overseeing such huge a framework requires the Operating system to be incredibly adaptable. Cloud Operating System is an open source web work area following the cloud figuring idea. It is principally written in PHP, XML, and JavaScript. It goes about as a stage for web applications composed utilizing the Cloud Computing ideas. It incorporates a Desktop condition with number of utilizations and framework utilities. It is open by compact gadgets by means of its portable front end. Each Cloud Operating System gives you a chance to transfer your documents what's more, work with them regardless of where you are. It contains applications like Word Processor, Address Book, pdf per user, and a lot increasingly created by the Cloud merchant. Cloud is a streamlined Operating System that runs just on a Web program, giving access to an assortment of electronic applications that enable the client to perform numerous basic undertakings without booting a full-scale Operating System. Due to its straight-forwardness, Cloud can boot in only a couple of moments. The Operating System is intended for Net books, Mobile Internet Gadgets, and PCs that are mostly used to peruse the internet. From cloud the client can rapidly boot into the fundamental OS, since cloud keeps booting the principle OS in the foundation.

A cloud operating system is a sort of operating system intended to work inside cloud processing and virtualization conditions. A cloud operating system deals with the activity, execution and procedures of virtual machines, virtual servers and virtual foundation, just as the back-end equipment and programming assets. A cloud operating system may likewise be known as a virtual operating system. A cloud operating system basically deals with the activity of at least one virtual machine inside a virtualized situation. Contingent upon the virtual condition and cloud benefits being used, the usefulness of cloud operating systems shifts.

Cloud OS Requirements

There are six basic requirements of cloud OS and is as follows:

- Cloud OS must allow self-sufficient administration of its assets in the interest of its clients and applications.
- Cloud OS activity must proceed in spite of loss of hubs, whole bunches, and system dividing.
- Cloud OS must be operating system and design skeptic.
- Cloud must help numerous sorts of uses, including inheritance
- Cloud OS the board framework must be decentralized, adaptable, have minimal overhead per client and per machine, and be financially savvy.
- The assets utilized in the Cloud engineering must be responsible, for example for charging and investigating purposes.

Cloud OS Architecture

The architecture of cloud operating system consists of four main components cloud server, cloud platform, cloud infrastructure and cloud storage.

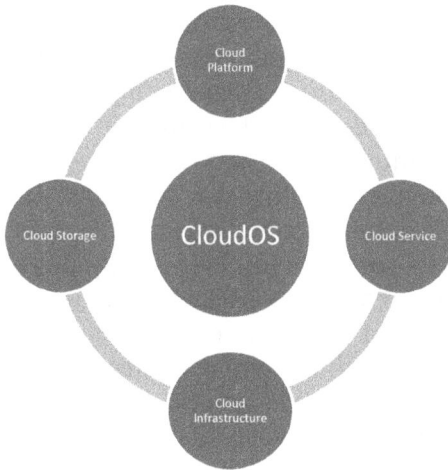

Figure 16. CloudOS architecture.

Goals of Cloud Operating System

- Having the option to work from all over the place, paying little respect to whether you are utilizing a full-included, present day PC, a versatile contraption, or a totally out of date PC.
- Sharing assets effectively between various work focuses at organization, or working from better places and nations on similar tasks.
- Continually getting a charge out of similar applications with a similar open arrangement, and overlooking the common similarity issues between office suites and conventional working frameworks.
- Having the option to keep working in the event that you need to leave your nearby PC or in the event that it just crashes, without losing information or time.

Different Types of Cloud Operating System

There are various cloud operating systems available some of which are listed below and as follows:

- **Ghost**: Ghost cloud computing is a main organization in the cloud computing industry spends significant time in cloud computing for the end client. Ghost offers people and organizations document stockpiling and applications in the cloud to empower secure individualized computing from any gadget. Ghost is dispersed straightforwardly from its site and through channels. Phantom web interface is exceptionally straightforward and simple to utilize, it make it fast and simple to deal with your documents and envelopes. We can transfer information of any sort to your cloud stockpiling from any gadget. We can see and alter any of your documents in any program. We can in a split second offer records and reports with any companion by sending them a connection. Any place you will be, you can alter archives and pictures legitimately online inside Ghost entry. It likewise offers full versatile help, you can peruse your document and folders from your cell gadget or we can mount as a Windows drive; simply like a USB blaze drive. We can move documents between neighborhood hard plate and your Cloud File.

- **Lucid**: Lucid heaps of utilizations. One can peruse photographs, tune in to music, and alter archives. It likewise accompanies a RSS channel per user, a few games, an adding machine, and a bash like terminal application.

- **Startforce**: With Startforce, we can run windows applications, for example, MS Office, Adobe Acrobat and Quickbooks. We can likewise line in web applications, for example, Salesforce.com, Google or your organization's intranet web applications.

- **Zimdesk**: Zimdesk is more of PC on the web. This consists of an internet browser and web association are all you have to get to your work area, records and most loved applications. You can get to your information whenever from anyplace, from any PC.

- **Glide**: Glide OS 4.0 is an extensive Ad-Free cloud computing arrangement. Clients who need additional capacity or might want to add additional clients can move up to Glide. The Glide OS gives programmed record and application similarity crosswise over gadgets and working frameworks. With Glide OS you likewise get the Glide Sync App which causes you to synchronize your home and work documents.

- **MyGoya**: MyGoya is a free web based working framework. Your very own work area can be gotten to from any Internet PC on the planet and incorporates email, visit, document sharing, schedule and a moment flag-bearer. Deal with your contacts from anyplace on the planet.

- **Amoeba**: This Cloud OS is a progressed online cloud operating system. Sign in to your free record and join a cloud computing insurgency that starts with extraordinary applications like Shutterborg, Exstream and Surf.

- **Cloudo**: This is a free Cloud Operating System that lives on the Internet, directly in your internet browser. This implies you can arrive at your archives, photographs, music and every single other record regardless of where you are, from any PC or cell phone. It includes an open, amazing, steady and flexible improvement condition. With the snap of a mouse button you can begin with making applications for yourself, a gathering of individuals or even everybody. What's more, on the off chance that we are great, we can make cash out of this also. We can undoubtedly share a lot of documents, pictures or set up a shared service with companions and partners.

- **Joli**: With this OS you never need to purchase another PC for at least a decade. It's simple an easy to install. Jump on the Web and right away interface with all your Web applications, records and administrations utilizing the PC you effectively claim.

- **Corneli**: The Corneli OS is a simple to utilize, multi-client and cross-program. Web Desktop Environment, Web Operating System or Web Office accompanies a lot of cool applications.

Benefits of the Cloud Operating System

- Worldwide accessibility of Cloud Operating Systems
- Requires just program.
- Dynamic substance and plan.
- Extensive rundown Applications.
- Remote storage.
- Browser and Platform autonomous.
- Rich word processing office

Summary

Cloud Operating System is an open source web work area following the cloud figuring idea. It is principally written in PHP, XML, and JavaScript. It goes about as a stage for web applications composed utilizing the cloud computing ideas. It incorporates a desktop condition with number of utilizations and framework utilities. It is open by compact gadgets by means of its portable front end. Each Cloud Operating System gives you a chance to transfer your documents what's more, work with them regardless of where you are. It contains applications like Word Processor, Address Book, pdf per user, and a lot increasingly created by the cloud merchant.

References

1. Chen, ZN, Chen, K, Jiang, JL., Evolution of Cloud Operating System: From Technology to Ecosystem, Journal of Computer Science and Technology, 32, 224-241, 2017, https://doi.org/10.1007/s11390-017-1717-z.
2. H. Musse, L. Alamro, Cloud Computing: Architecture and Operating System, Global Summit on Computer and Information Technology, Sousse, Tunisia, Pages. 3-8, 2016, DOI: 10.1109/GSCIT.2016.7.

Further Readings

1. The 15 Best Cloud OS to Use in 2020: The Experts' Recommendation (ubuntupit.com)

5

Management in Cloud Computing

Learning Objectives

- Understanding service level agreement in cloud
- To learn billing and accounting principles of cloud
- Give a brief description of charging models in cloud
- Describing data management suitable for cloud

Cloud management alludes to the advancements and programming that are intended for working and checking applications, information and administrations that dwell in the cloud. Cloud management apparatuses ensure that an organization's cloud assets are working appropriately and monitored, in this way enabling directors to rather concentrate on supporting other center business forms. Cloud management systems ordinarily include various errands including execution checking (reaction times, dormancy, uptime, and so forth.), security and consistence inspecting and management, and starting and administering catastrophe recuperation and alternate courses of action. The absolute best cloud management frameworks mechanize the choices and procedure of provisioning different assets against assorted approaching remaining burdens. In this manner, organizations can appreciate a quicker conveyance of IT administrations to organizations; decreased capital and working expenses; and mechanized chargeback for asset use and revealing, Moreover, cloud management arrangements can guarantee that the continually developing number of IT administrations won't bomb so IT staff can scale without stress just as meet assistance level prerequisites and address evolving conditions.

Characteristics of Cloud Management

- Support of various cloud types
- Creation and provisioning of various cloud assets, e.g., machine occurrences, stockpiling, or organized applications
- Performance announcing including accessibility and uptime, reaction time, asset amount use and different attributes

- The formation of dashboards that can be tweaked for a specific customer's needs 50 Tivoli Service Automation Manager is a case of a structure instrument for overseeing cloud framework.
- Delivers a higher level of institutionalization and computerization for sending and management of IT administrations while saving gifted IT staff part's the ideal opportunity for other high-esteem errands
- Provides detectable procedures and endorsement routings to fill in as review trails, and incorporates with process administration
- Offers an incorporated management ability that locations the lifecycle changes of a cloud administration
- Provides versatile and robotized best rehearses for building and overseeing IT frameworks
- A structure based upon Tivoli's administration management stage, utilizing existing interests in administration management abilities

Service Level Agreement

Analysts characterized Service Level Agreement as a configuration that contains a clarification of the concurred administration, parameters of the degree of administration, the certifications in regards to the Quality of Service, and plans for all instances of infringement. The SLA is noteworthy as an agreement that is held between the supplier of the administration and another gathering who could be one of following; customer of the administration, intermediary moderator, or checking mediator. The key idea of SLA is to give an unmistakable portrayal of the official understandings about assistance articulations, for example, execution, accessibility and charging and so on. It is fundamental that the SLA ought to contain the obligations and the exercises that will be done in the event of any negation. So this agreement decides, ordinarily in quantifiable terms, the administrations that the specialist co-op will give and what endorse the Service Provider will pay if the devoted targets can't be met. SLA has been applied in an assortment of spaces that are identified with IT, for example, Web Services, Networking, Internet, and Data Center Management; the current portrayals contrast from area to space.

The cloud customer is the individual with an intrigue or worry for the cloud registering administration. A cloud customer represents an individual or organization that adventures the administration from a cloud provider. A cloud customer investigates the administration list from a cloud provider, requests the best possible assistance, and establishes administration shows with the cloud provider. The cloud client can be approached to pay for the administration provided, and to compose costs thusly. Cloud clients require SLAs to recognize the specialized exhibition requests fulfilled by a cloud provider. SLAs can achieve conditions about the prevalence of administration, security, and remedies for the confronting breakdowns. A cloud provider could likewise state in the SLAs a gathering of ensures that are not set up to clients obviously, for example limitations, and obligations that cloud clients need to support on. A cloud client can choose a cloud provider with best valuing and increasingly complimentary conditions. Regularly, a cloud provider's valuing methodology and SLAs are non-discussable, with the exception of if the client anticipates concentrated business and can have the option to examine for predominant show. Depending on the administrations requested, the activities and business circumstances can be various over cloud clients.

The customers of SaaS may be partnerships that offer their members with access to programming applications, end customers who quickly misuse programming applications, or programming application executives who comprise applications for the customers. SaaS costs can be paid by the quantity of the end customers, the utilization time, the system transfer speed spent, the amount of data kept or the time of keeping data.

Cloud customers of PaaS can misuse the instruments and the assets provided by cloud providers to advance, look at, introduce and regulate the applications displayed in a cloud medium. PaaS customers can be application fashioners who create and achieve application programming. Likewise, they can be application analyst who execute and look at applications in cloud-based areas. They can be application distributers who appropriate applications through the cloud, or can be application administrators who comprise and control applications. PaaS costs can be paid dependent on, activity, database space, arrange assets utilized by the PaaS application, or the time of the stage show.

Customers of IaaS have a passage to virtual registering machines, organize putting away space, arrange foundation components, and other fundamental assets on which they can introduce and work irregular programming. The customers of IaaS can be framework architects or framework directors who are worried in making, running, sorting out and controlling administrations for IT basis forms. IaaS clients are given the capacities to enter these assets, and are paid relying upon the amount or time span of the assets utilized like; CPU hours devoured by virtual figuring machines, limit, organize data transfer capacity utilized, and amount of IP tends to used for specific periods.

Advantages

- **Improved client acknowledgment level**: A clearly clarified SLA extends the client endorsement level, as it bolsters suppliers to focus on the client needs and affirms that the work is set on the correct way.
- **Enhanced connection between the gatherings**: A conspicuous SLA determines the compensation and requital strategies of the administration gave. The shopper can look at administrations as indicated by Service Level Objectives (SLO) decided in the SLA. Also, the particular agreement helps gatherings to explain differences without trouble.
- **Enhanced service quality**: Each component in a SLA suits a Key Performance Indicators (KPI) that decides the client assistance among an internal organization by checking whether these markers coordinate the Service Level Objectives (SLOs) of the concurred agreement among clients and specialist co-ops. An agreement is a method for explaining the distinction in requirements for both the supplier and the client. A SLO consistently contains level administrations, explicit period, and a particular esteem as an objective to accomplish. These genuine presentation esteems are contrasted and the expressed ones in the agreement to make execution reports utilized for assessment .The key for arriving at the ideal degree of value is to choose the quality markers in the beginning periods to utilize them later in deciding infringement. SLA formats and components can be portrayed dependent on their presentation, accessibility, and adaptation to non-critical failure.

- **Performance**: It is characterized by the reaction time. QoS metric which alludes to the most extreme time that the solicitation treatment can take from the hour of capacity, and the appearance of the reaction. At the point when a client has an arrangement or agreement for the specialist organization, at that point the supplier interprets and decides the reaction time contingent upon its necessities. From that point forward, the specialist organization gets administration assets from the foundation during entire term of agreement. The prerequisites are utilized to choose and build up the administration occasion

- **Fault eesistance**: It is characterized by the unwavering quality of the framework which alludes to the level of trustworthiness. Adaptation to non-critical failure QoS affirmation system is fundamentally utilized by the specialist organization to catch and oppose blames or crashes during the treatment. These shortcomings can be delegated either work disappointments or occupation delays. A fruitless activity execution can be named work disappointment. To decide a vocation delay, some supplier's data should be referred to, for example, execution time of the activity and solicitation reaction time. At last, by illuminating the deferred employments during the solicitation treatment, adaptation to internal failure is ensured.

Billing and Accounting

Billing is the way toward figuring out what a specialist organization will get from an end client in return for giving their administrations. The billing procedure can be as per the following: fixed, in which the client is charged a similar sum constantly; dynamic, in which the value charged changes powerfully; or advertise subordinate, in which the client is charged dependent on the ongoing economic situations. Fixed valuing systems incorporate the pay per-utilize model, in which the clients pay for the sum they expend of an item or the measure of time they utilize a specific assistance. Membership is another kind of fixed estimating, in which the client pays a fixed measure of cash to utilize the administration for longer periods at any helpful time or sum. A rundown cost is another type of fixed estimating, in which a fixed cost is found in an inventory or a rundown. Then again, differential or dynamic estimating suggests that the value changes progressively as indicated by the administration highlights, client qualities, measure of bought volumes, or client inclinations. Market dependent estimating, nonetheless, relies upon the constant economic situations, for example, bartering, selling, demand conduct, and yields the executives.

Following are the most appropriate variables that impact valuing in distributed computing:

- **Initial costs**: This is the measure of cash that the specialist organization spends every year to purchase assets.
- **Lease period**: This is the period where the client will rent assets from the specialist co-op. Specialist co-ops typically offer lower unit costs for longer membership periods.
- **QoS**: This is the arrangement of advances and systems offered by the specialist organization to improve the client involvement with the cloud, for example, information protection and asset accessibility. The better QoS offered, the higher the cost will be. Universal Journal of Grid and Distributed Computing.
- **Age of assets**: This is the age of the assets utilized by the specialist organization. The more seasoned the assets are, the lower the value charged will be. This is on the grounds that assets can continue wear after some time, which lessens their monetary worth.
- **Cost of support**: This is the measure of cash that the specialist organization spends on keeping up and verifying the cloud annually.

Requirements of Effective Billing

A truly cloud-centric billing system needs to support the following services:

- **Complex items**: Cloud computing items can be as basic or as mind boggling as the client requires. Cloud specialist organizations need a framework that can bolster as a lot of multifaceted nature as they decide to give.
- **Scalability**: The sheer volume of individual things that a cloud specialist organization needs to charge is critical. It will likewise keep on developing quickly as each new help is brought to advertise and the client base expands.
- **Real-time**: In the event that the clouds can arrangement new

administrations in a flash, at that point the billing framework needs to keep up. And with new items, costs, cross-item advancements, basic offers or new bundles to consider, the billing framework needs to keep up continuous information on all costs at the hour of billing. One approach to guarantee a troubled client is to create a receipt that doesn't mirror the advancement the client thought they were exploiting.

- **Self-administration provisioning**: Clients need to realize what they're going to pay in advance, and your billing framework should have the option to follow each time they arrangement another help, check it against current costs and any joint advancements, and create a receipt appropriately.

- **Visibility and control**: In an public, private or hybrid cloud condition, specialist organizations need total perceivability over how their assets are being utilized, so they can bill or screen adequately. Before the cloud, how your assets were being utilized was commonly substantially more imperceptible to you, yet this was not an issue as clients consented to pay fixed sums every month. With cloud billing, you can take the utility model and straightforwardness of the cloud and make it beneficial.

- **Granular billing**: With such a large number of parts making up a cloud administration, the billing framework should be granular enough to penetrate down into every segment or administration and report this back to the client as and when they need it.

Issues in Cloud Billing

- **Malicious insider**: Malicious insider is a present or previous worker, contractual worker, or different colleague who has or had approved access to an association's system, framework, or information and purposefully surpassed or abused that entrance in a way that contrarily influenced the classification, uprightness, or accessibility of the association's data or data frameworks.

- **Multi-cloud contributions**: Managed cloud administrations can help with different prerequisites too. The key is to discover an overseen cloud supplier that can give a solitary purpose of the board for different clouds. This requires applications that conceal the usage subtleties of key usefulness, similar to account the board and access control implementation. For instance, an oversaw cloud supplier that can incorporate with your on premise Active Directory or LDAP support and apply that to applications running in various clouds can spare you a lot of the board.

- **Authentication and information encryption**: The Authentication and information encryption rely upon clients having and overseeing encryption keys. An over cloud supplier can help keep up security and decrease the danger of losing information with key the board support. Keep in mind, in the event that you scramble your information and lose the encryption key, at that point your information is basically difficult to reach. In the event that various workers share obligation regarding putting away encoded information, at that point a unified key administration can help keep up steady practices with respect to securing encryption keys. PKI based validation system are excessively exorbitant, so light weight confirmation component are favoured for verification.

- **Integrity in billing transaction**: For straightforward charging of the cloud benefits, each charging exchange ought to be ensured against falsification and bogus alterations. Albeit business CSP, furnish clients with administration charging records and keeping in mind that few specialists have exhibited asset utilization preparing frameworks that record the utilization of lattice assets, they can't give a dependable review trail. It is on the grounds that the client or the CSP can alter the charging records considerably after a shared understanding between the client and the CSP, prompting the contest between them. For this situation, even an outsider can't affirm that the client's record is right or that the CSP's record is right.

- **Billing exchange**: Cloud administration clients and CSPs can produce countless charging exchanges on the grounds that on-request cloud benefits progressively scale their ability upwards or downwards. For instance, on account of iCubeCloud which is the hidden cloud figuring foundation of this investigation), the charging recurrence per client of the main 15 percent substantial clients is regularly around 4,200 charging exchanges for each day. They periodically create in excess of 200 charging exchanges for each second, as they as a rule conjure enormously parallel procedures in a buxom way. The successive charging exchanges lead to inordinate computational overhead for both the CSP and the client when the previously mentioned security highlight is associated with the charging exchange. Thusly, the overhead forced by the charging exchange should be inside adequate cut off points in order to be appropriate to a wide range of figuring gadgets, for example, advanced mobile phones, tablets, note pads, and work area PCs.

- **Trusted SLA checking**: Once a cloud administration client and CSP concur on a SLA, the administration quality ought to be observed in a trusted manner. A CSP may convey a screen and make the screen's usefulness accessible to its clients. Be that as it may, the nearness of the screen itself is lacking on the grounds that the screens are sent on cloud assets that are not worked by clients. The CSP may intentionally or accidentally create off base observing records, bringing about inaccurate bills. To give a SLA checking system, a few examinations have tried incredible endeavours to structure arrangements that meet different necessities, incorporating versatility with circulated asset observing, information stream observing, and expectations of SLA infringement, as opposed to tending to security concerns, for example, the respectability and reliability of the checking component. In this way, they are not completely steady of the security issues.

- **Scalability**: Scalability is a key necessity for CSPs in the present advertise, regardless of whether it is to help the quantity of new endorsers and gadgets that are propelled or the quantity of new accomplices, substance and plans of action that will adapt these or the systems that are supporting them. Redknee sees that so as to expand this new time of versatility, CSPs should likewise be outfitted with more noteworthy deftness, which is the place we see the cloud assuming a more prominent job.

Scaling Hardware: Traditional Vs. Cloud

While thinking about the financial parts of moving to the cloud, the best spot to start is by looking at the expense of an on-premise server versus a cloud server. The expense for an organization with in excess of 50 workers to run an on-premise server for a time of around five to seven years is normally short of what it would be for utilizing a cloud server. Then again, on the off chance that the server just keeps going a few years, at that point cloud registering is considerably more financially savvy. Different components to consider are the aberrant expenses of running your own servers, for example, cooling, control, permit charges, and work.

These are the most well-known reasons associations are persuaded to move away from customary IT towards cloud figuring.

- Cost Savings and Total Cost of Ownership. At the point when you move to cloud processing you will in general set aside cash in a few different ways in contrast with conventional IT, incorporating the decrease of in-house hardware and framework.
- Dissatisfaction in Traditional IT. Numerous organizations are disappointed with the negatives that accompany conventional IT, for example, poor information reinforcement, overseeing and keeping up your very own equipment, and absence of fiasco recuperation choices. Organizations regularly become disappointed that they don't have a similar limit, versatility, and adaptability as the individuals who are utilizing the cloud. You likewise don't have a similar access to applications and information.
- Time to Value and Ease of Implementation. Since you don't need to invest energy designing equipment, look after frameworks, and fixing programming, you can contribute your assets somewhere else.
- Access to Emerging Technology. Much like a vehicle, the moment you buy on-premise equipment and programming, it promptly begins to age. You can get to the best in class developments with a cloud supplier who has all the more acquiring force and keeps awake to-date with accessible arrangements. Additionally, as new advancements are discharged, they become less inclined to incorporate with heritage arrangements that are frequently resolute. Rather, cloud-first improvement is going to the bleeding edge.
- Using Hybrid to Optimize your Operations. A few associations take the utilization of the cloud significantly further by utilizing different clouds at the same time, along these lines giving them much greater spryness. Remaining tasks at hand are put where they perform best, and where expenses are generally proficient.

Charging Models

- **Pricing models**: Unending pricing in this model, the expense to possess an advertising is determined in advance and charged to the licensee consequently to a ceaseless (always) right to utilize the advertising. In web based business programming contributions, there is now and again a required yearly upkeep cost included to offer help on the advertising. This model as a rule is reasonable for undertakings with additional capital.

- **Leasing**: Renting an asset includes paying an arranged cost to have the asset over some time period, whether or not you utilize the asset.

- **Membership based pricing**: This is the most broadly utilized estimating model for SaaS. This model enables the clients to anticipate their occasional costs of utilizing the cloud applications. Be that as it may, it comes up short on the exactness of charging the clients for what they really have utilized.

- **Pay-more only as costs arise**: Pay-as-you-go includes metering use and charging dependent on genuine use, freely of the timeframe over which the use happens. Amazon gathers together their charging to the closest server-hour or gigabyte-month, yet the related dollar sums are little enough to make it a genuine pay-more only as costs arise administration.

- **Layered pricing**: Tiered estimating is the model received by Amazon's cloud frameworks, where the cloud administrations are offered in a few levels; every level offers fixed processing details and SLA at a particular value for every unit time.

- **Saved instances**: Amazon's held cases give shoppers the alternative to make a low, once installment for each occurrence you need to save and thus get a noteworthy markdown on the hourly charge for that example. There are three saved Instance types (Light, Medium, and Heavy Use Reserved Instances) that empower buyers to adjust the sum you pay forthright with your successful hourly cost. Saved Instances can be bought legitimately from Amazon for 1 or multiyear terms. Utilizing the Reserved Instance Commercial center, you have the adaptability to buy Reserved Occurrences from Amazon Reserved Instance Marketplace Sellers for terms going between multi months to three years (depending on accessible choice). In either case, the one-time expense per occurrence is non-refundable.

- **Light and medium utilization**: Reserved Instances additionally are charged by the occurrence hour for the time that examples are in a running state; if purchasers don't run the occasion in 60 minutes, there is zero use charge. Incomplete example hours devoured are charged as entire hours. Overwhelming Utilization Reserved Instances are charged for consistently during the whole Reserved Instance term (which implies shoppers are charged the hourly expense in any case of whether any use has happened during 60 minutes).
- **Spot instances**: Spot instances empower purchasers to offer for unused Amazon EC2 limit. Occurrences are charged the Spot Price, which is set by Amazon EC2 and changes intermittently relying upon the stockpile of and interest for Spot Occasion limit. To utilize Spot Instances, buyers place a Spot Instance demand, indicating the occurrence type, the Accessibility Zone wanted, the quantity of Spot Instances to be run, and the most extreme value that customer is willing to pay per occurrence hour. To decide how that most extreme cost analyzes to past Spot Prices, the Spot Price history is accessible through the Amazon EC2 API and the AWS Management Console. In the event that customer's greatest value offer surpasses the present Spot Value, your solicitation is satisfied and the buyer's examples will run until either buyer decides to end them or the Spot Price increments over the present most extreme cost.
- **On demand instances**: Amazon's on-request occurrences let purchasers pay for register limit constantly with no long haul responsibilities. This liberates customers from the expenses what's more, complexities of arranging, acquiring, and keeping up equipment and changes what are ordinarily huge fixed expenses into a lot littler variable expenses.
- **Per-unit pricing**: Per-Unit pricing is ordinarily applied to information moves or memory use. Principle memory allotment, for instance is utilized by GoGrid Cloud offering, where they indicated RAM/hour as the use unit for their framework. This model is, seemingly more adaptable than the layered estimating, as it enables the clients to modify the principle memory allotment of their framework dependent on their particular applications needs.

- **Variable pricing model**: Herein the evaluating depends on the level of interest of a specific asset type, daytime versus evening, weekdays versus ends of the week, spot costs, thus forward. The diverse group hubs can change powerfully their areas, starting with one cloud supplier then onto the next one, so as to decrease the general foundation cost.
- **Cloud option pricing model**: This is a model that uses budgetary alternative hypothesis to all the while moderate chance and limit cost for cloud clients. One of the essential fundamental standards in numerical money is the Efficient Market Hypothesis which expresses that stock costs effectively fuse all accessible data. Something else unsurprising value developments would produce potential outcomes for examiners to pick up chance free benefits. In effective markets, such examiners consistently exist and they generally exploit the displayed chances, subsequently at last all such openings have been taken and all accessible data has been fused into the present market cost.

Load Balancing

Load balancing is a system that helped systems and assets by giving a maximum throughput least reaction time. Load balancing is isolating the traffic between all servers, so information can be sent and got immediately with load balancing. In cloud condition numerous calculations are accessible that aides in appropriate rush hour gridlock Loaded between every single accessible server. A large portion of them can be applied in the cloud condition with reasonable checks.

Load balancing can be arranged into static load balancing calculation and dynamic load balancing calculation:

Static approach: This methodology is for the most part characterized in the plan or usage of the framework. Static load balancing calculations partition the traffic proportionately between all servers.

Dynamic approach: This methodology considered just the present condition of the framework during load balancing choices. Dynamic approach is increasingly reasonable for generally circulated frameworks, for example, distributed computing.

Metrics for Load Balancing

- **Throughput**: It is utilized to compute the all undertakings whose execution has been finished. The exhibition of any framework is improved if throughput is high.
- **Fault tolerance**: It implies recuperation from disappointment. The load balancing ought to be a decent fault tolerant strategy.
- **Relocation time**: It is an ideal opportunity to move the employments or assets from one hub to different hubs. It is ought to be limited so as to upgrade the presentation of the framework.
- **Response Time**: It is the measure of time that is taken by a specific load balancing calculation to reaction an undertaking in a framework. This parameter ought to be limited for better execution of a framework.
- **Scalability**: It is the capacity of a calculation to perform load balancing for any limited number of hubs of a framework. This measurement ought to be improved for a decent framework.

Policies of Load Balancing Algorithm

Numerous strategies are utilized in load balancing algorithms:

- **Information policy**: It characterizes what data is required and how this data is gathered.
- **Triggering policy**: This characterizes the timeframe when the heap adjusting activity is beginning to deal with the heap.
- **Resource type policy**: This policy characterizes a wide range of assets which are accessible during the heap adjusting.
- **Location policy**: This uses every one of the after effects of the asset type policy. It is utilized to discover an accomplice for a server or recipient.
- **Selection policy**: This policy is utilized to discover the errand which moves from over-burden hub to free hub.

Major goals of Load Balancing Algorithm

- **Cost adequacy**: Load balancing help in give better framework execution at lower cost.

- **Versatility and adaptability**: The framework for which load balancing calculations are executed might be change in measure after some time. So the calculation must deal with these sorts' circumstances. So calculation must be adaptable and versatile.
- **Priority**: Prioritization of the assets or occupations should be finished. So higher need occupations show signs of improvement opportunity to execute.

Existing Load Balancing Algorithm

There are many load balancing algorithms which help to achieve better throughput and improve the response time in cloud environment. All the algorithms have their own benefits.

- **Task scheduling based on LB**: This calculation essentially comprises two level assignment booking component which depend on load balancing to meet powerful prerequisites of clients. It gets high asset use. This calculation accomplishes load balancing by first mapping assignments to virtual machines and afterward all virtual machines to have assets. It is improving the assignment reaction time. It additionally gives better asset usage.
- **Opportunistic load balancing**: OLB is to endeavour every hub keeps occupied, accordingly doesn't consider the present workload of every PC. OLB allocates each errand in free request to display hub of valuable. The preferred position is very straightforward and arrive at load balance yet its inadequacy isn't consider every desire execution time of undertaking, hence the entire function time is poor.
- **Round robin**: In this calculation every one of the procedures are partitioned between all processors. In this each procedure is allotted to the processor in a cooperative request. The outstanding task at hand appropriations between processors are equivalent. Various forms have not same work handling time. At many times a few hubs might be intensely loaded and others stay inert In web servers where http demands are of comparative nature and dispersed similarly then RR calculation is utilized. In Round Robin Scheduling the time quantum assume a significant job. At the point when time quantum is exceptionally enormous then RR Scheduling Algorithm is same as

the FCFS Scheduling. Furthermore, when time quantum is too little at that point Round Robin Scheduling is known as Processor Sharing Algorithm.

- **Randomized**: This calculation is static in nature. In this calculation a procedure can be taken care of by a specific hub n with a likelihood p. At the point when every one of the procedures are of equivalent loaded then this calculation function admirably. Issue emerges when loads are of various computational complexities. This calculation isn't keeping up deterministic methodology.

- **Min-min algorithm**: It begins with a lot of every single unassigned assignment. In this base fruition time for all undertakings is found. At that point after that among these base occasions the base worth is chosen. At that point task with least time plan on machine. After that the execution time for every other undertaking is refreshed on that machine on the other hand a similar method is pursued until every one of the errands allocated on the assets. The fundamental issue of this calculation is has a starvation.

- **Max-min algorithm**: Max-Min calculation is practically same as the min-min calculation. The fundamental distinction is following: In this calculation first discovering least execution times, at that point the greatest worth is chosen which is the most extreme time among every one of the assignments on any asset. After that greatest time finding, the undertaking is doled out on the specific chose machine. Then the execution time for all errands is refreshed on that machine, this is finished by including the execution time of the doled out undertaking to the execution times of different assignments on that machine. At that point all relegated undertaking is expelled from the rundown that executed by the framework.

- **Honeybee foraging behavior**: It is a nature roused Algorithm for self-association. Bumble bee accomplishes worldwide load balancing through neighborhood server activities. The exhibition of the framework is upgraded with expanded framework decent variety. The fundamental issue is that throughput isn't expanded with an expansion in framework size. At the point when the various populace of administration types is required then this calculation is most appropriate.

- **Active clustering**: In this calculation same type hubs of the framework are assembled and they cooperate in gatherings. It works like as self-conglomeration load balancing strategy where a system is revamped to adjust the load of the framework. Frameworks upgrade utilizing comparative employment assignments by associating comparable administrations. Framework Performance improved with improved assets. The throughput is improved by utilizing every one of these assets viably.

- **Compare and balance**: This calculation is utilizations to arrive at a harmony condition and oversee lopsided frameworks load. In this calculation based on likelihood, current host arbitrarily select a host and think about their load. On the off chance that load of current host is more than chose host, it moves additional load to that specific hub. At that point each host of the framework plays out a similar strategy. This load balancing calculation is likewise planned and actualized to lessen virtual machines relocation time. Common stockpiling memory is utilized to decrease virtual machines movement time.

- **Lock-free multiprocessing solution**: It proposed a sans lock multiprocessing load balancing arrangement that stays away from the utilization of shared memory rather than other multiprocessing load balancing arrangements which utilize shared memory and lock to keep up a client session. It is accomplished by adjusting portion. This arrangement helps in improving the general execution of load balancer in a multicore domain by running various load-balancing forms in a single load balancer.

- **Ant colony optimization**: An Ant calculation is a multiagent way to deal with troublesome combinatorial enhancement issues. Case of this methodology is travelling salesman problem (TSP) and the quadratic assignment problem (QAP). These calculations were motivated by the perception of genuine insect states.

- **Shortest response time first**: The possibility of this calculation is straight forward. In this each procedure is allotted a need which is permitted to run. In this equivalent need forms are booked in FCFS request. The (SJF) calculation is a unique instance of general need Scheduling calculation. In SJF calculation is need is the backwards of the following CPU burst. That is to say, on the off chance that more drawn out the CPU burst, at that point brings down the need. The SJF approach chooses the activity with the most brief (expected) preparing time first. In this calculation shorter occupations are executed after a short time employment. In SJF, it is critical to know or gauge the handling time of each activity which is serious issue of SJF.

- **Based random sampling:** This calculation depends on the development of the virtual chart having availability between the all hubs of the framework where every hub of the diagram is comparing to the hub PC of the cloud framework. Edges between hubs are two sorts as Incoming edge and active edge that is utilized to think about the load of specific framework and furthermore allocation the assets of the hub. It is excellent procedure to adjust the load.

Data Management

Data management applications are potential possibility for organization in the cloud industry: undertaking database framework have huge in advance cost that incorporates both equipment and programming costs the scholarly community: oversee, process and offer mass-delivered data in the cloud. Many Cloud Killer Apps are in certainty data-serious: Batch Processing likewise with map/diminish Online Transaction Processing (OLTP) as in computerized business applications Offline Analytical Processing (OLAP) as in data mining or AI.

Data Management in the cloud are categorized into two types:

Type-1: Transactional based data management by Transactional based data management, we allude to the bread-and-butter of the database business, databases that back banking, aircraft reservation, online web-based business, and store network management applications. These applications commonly depend on the ACID ensures that databases give, and will in general be decently compose concentrated.

Type-2: Analytical data management by Analytical data management, we allude to applications that question a data store for use in business arranging, critical thinking, and choice support. Recorded data alongside data from different operational databases are for the most part normally associated with the investigation.

Viewing at Data, Scalability & Cloud Services

Scalability is the capacity of a procedure, system, programming or machine to develop and oversee expanded requests. This is one of the most significant and prevalent component of cloud computing. Through scalability you can scale up your information stockpiling limit or downsize it to satisfy the needs of your developing business. Scaling in the cloud gives you the best understanding of adaptability of time and cash for your business. At the point when business requests are expanding, you can without much of a stretch add hubs to build your extra room, or you can expand the quantity of servers as of now utilized. At the point when the expanded interest is decreased then you can move back to your unique arrangement.

Scalability empowers you to oblige bigger remaining tasks at hand without interruption or complete change of existing framework. To adequately use scalability, you have to comprehend the unpredictability and the kinds of scalability.

Three types of scalability - Vertical, Horizontal and Diagonal.

Scale Vertically - Scale Up

Vertical Scaling or Scaling up is simple, it tends to be finished by moving the application to greater virtual machines conveyed in the cloud or you can scale up by including extension units also with your present foundation. This capacity to add assets to suit expanding remaining burden volumes is vertical scaling. It can resize your server with no adjustment in your code. The drawback to scaling up is that it builds stockpiling limit yet the presentation is diminished in light of the fact that the register limit continues as before. Outstanding tasks at hand requiring higher throughput request decreased idleness and this can just by satisfied by Horizontal Scaling/Scaling out.

Scale Horizontally - Scale out

Horizontal Scaling or scaling out is the option of hubs to the current foundation to oblige extra outstanding burden volumes. As opposed to Vertical Scaling, Horizontal Scaling additionally conveys execution alongside capacity limit.

The complete remaining task at hand volume is collected over the all-out number of hubs and inertness is adequately decreased. This scaling is perfect for remaining burdens that require diminished inactivity and advanced throughput.

Scale Diagonally

Diagonal scaling causes you join the scaling up and downsizing. As the term recommends, downsizing is the evacuation of capacity assets as necessities decline. Slanting scaling conveys adaptability for outstanding task at hand that require extra stockpiling assets for explicit occasions of time. For example, a site sets up corner to corner scaling; as the traffic builds, the process prerequisites are suited. As the traffic diminishes, the calculation limit is re-established to its unique size.

This sort of scaling presents upgraded planning, cost adequacy for situations and organizations managing variable remaining burden volumes.

Scalable Cloud Based Services

- Infrastructure-as-a-Service (IaaS)
- Platform-as-a-Service (PaaS)
- Storage-as-a-Service (STaaS)
- Data-as-a-Service (DaaS)
- Database-as-a-Service (DBaaS)

Advantages of Cloud Scalability

- **Performance**: One centre advantage of scalability in the cloud is that it encourages execution. Adaptable engineering can deal with the eruptions of traffic and substantial remaining tasks at hand that will accompany the business development setup.
- **Cost-proficient**: You can enable your business to develop without rolling out any costly improvements in the present arrangement. This decreases the cost ramifications of capacity development making scalability in the cloud financially savvy.
- **Simple and quick**: Scaling up or scaling out in the cloud is less complex; you can commission extra VMs with a couple of

snaps and after the instalment is prepared, the extra assets are accessible immediately.

- **Capacity**: Scalability guarantees that with the persistent development of your business the extra room in cloud develops too. Adaptable distributed computing frameworks suit your information development prerequisites. With scalability, you don't need to stress over extra limit needs.
- **Scalability admonishment**: Scalability additionally has a few impediments. In the event that you need a completely adaptable framework, at that point you have an enormous errand to deal with. It requires arranging, testing and again testing for your information stockpiling. In the event that you have the applications effectively, at that point separating the framework will require code changes, refreshes what's more, checking. You must be solid and steady for the computerized change of your foundation.

Database and Data Stores in Cloud

A cloud database is an assortment of instructive substance, either organized or unstructured, that dwells on a private, open or cross breed distributed computing foundation stage. From a basic and structure point of view, a cloud database is the same than one that works without anyone else on-premises servers. The basic contrast lies in where the database lives.

Where an on-premises database is associated with nearby clients through a partnership's inner neighborhood, a cloud database lives on servers and capacity outfitted by a cloud or database as a help (DBaaS) supplier and it is gotten to exclusively through the web. To a product application, for instance, a SQL database dwelling on-premises or in the cloud ought to seem indistinguishable.

The conduct of the database ought to be a similar whether gotten to through direct inquiries, for example, SQL explanations, or through API calls. Nonetheless, it might be conceivable to recognize little contrasts accordingly time. An on-premises database, got to with a LAN, is probably going to give a marginally quicker reaction than a cloud-based database, which requires a full circle on the web for every co-operation with the database.

How Cloud Databases Work

Cloud databases, similar to their customary progenitors, can be isolated into two general classes: social and non-relational.

A social database, normally written in Structured Query Language (SQL), is made out of a lot of interrelated tables that are sorted out into lines and sections. The connection among tables and segments (fields) is determined in a composition. SQL databases, by configuration, depend on information that is exceptionally steady in its arrangement, for example, banking exchanges or a phone catalog. Prominent cloud stages and cloud suppliers incorporate MySQL, Oracle, IBM DB2 and Microsoft SQL Server. Some cloud stages, for example, MySQL are publicly released.

Nonrelational databases, here and there called NoSQL, don't utilize a table model. Rather, they store content, paying little mind to its structure, as a solitary record. This innovation is appropriate for unstructured information, for example, online life content, photographs and recordings.

Types of Cloud Databases

Two cloud database condition models exist: Traditional and database as a service (DBaaS). In a traditional cloud model, a database runs on an IT division's framework with a virtual machine. Assignments of database oversight and the board fall upon IT staff members of the association.

The DBaaS model is an expense-based membership administration in which the database runs on the specialist organization's physical framework. Distinctive help levels are generally accessible. In a great DBaaS plan, the supplier keeps up the physical foundation and database, leaving the client to deal with the database's substance and activity.

On the other hand, a client can set up an oversaw facilitating plan, in which the supplier handles database support and the board. This last alternative might be particularly appealing to independent ventures that have database needs yet need sufficient IT mastery.

Cloud Database Benefits

Contrasted and working a customary database on an on location physical server and capacity engineering, a cloud database offers the accompanying particular focal points:

- **Elimination of physical framework**: In a cloud database condition, the cloud registering supplier of servers, stockpiling and other foundation is answerable for support and keeping high accessibility. The association that claims and works the database is answerable for supporting and keeping up the database programming and its substance. In a DBaaS situation, the specialist co-op is answerable for overseeing and working the database programming, leaving the DBaaS clients mindful just for their own information.
- **Cost investment funds**: Through the disposal of a physical framework possessed and worked by an IT office, huge reserve funds can be accomplished from diminished capital consumptions, less staff, diminished electrical and HVAC working expenses and a littler measure of required physical space.
- DBaaS benefits additionally incorporate prompt versatility, execution ensures, failover support, declining evaluating and concentrated aptitude.

Migrating Legacy Databases to the Cloud

An on-premises database can move to a cloud usage. Various reasons exist for doing this, including the accompanying:

- Allows IT to resign on-premises physical server and capacity framework.
- Fills the ability hole when IT needs sufficient in-house database aptitude.
- Improves handling effectiveness, particularly when applications and examination dwell in the cloud.
- Achieves cost investment funds through a few methods, including:
  - Reduction of in-house IT staff.
  - Continually declining cloud administration valuing.
  - Paying for just the assets devoured, referred to as pay-more only as costs arise evaluating.

Moving a database to the cloud can be a compelling method to additionally empower business application execution as a feature of a more extensive programming as-an administration organization. Doing so disentangles the procedures required to make data accessible through web-based associations. Capacity solidification can likewise be an advantage of moving an organization's databases to the cloud. Databases in various branches of an enormous organization, for instance, can be joined in the cloud into a solitary facilitated database the executive's framework.

Large Scale Data Processing

It is hard to deal with the information created in the web, IT frameworks, and so on (e.g., exchange logs, sensor logs, and life logs) and other information that keeps on expanding dangerously in volume. Examination of such voluminous information (known as large information) in a traditional way turns out to be exponentially expensive in any event, when the information is gathered by the framework, so the information has been either put away inefficiently or disposed of. The approach of scale-out innovation, be that as it may, has diminished the expense of building frameworks for preparing large-scale information, and new propelled administrations, for example, personalization dependent on investigative outcomes are presently conceivable.

Large-scale information handling empowers the utilization of different sorts of huge information in a cloud situation so as to make crush up administrations. A large-scale dispersed information preparing stage gathers and stores the enormous information delivered by IT frameworks or the Internet. By breaking down such large volumes of information, one can procure new information and skill and make new blend administrations. A large-scale circulated information handling stage is relied upon to fill in as a stage for making information on which to base propelled administrations for clients.

Summary

Cloud Management is one of the important concepts that describe the way in which the cloud is managed. It includes operations such as service level agreement, billing and accounting, charging models etc., are managed in cloud. This chapter also provides insights regarding load balancing and management of data in cloud starting from data viewing to processing.

References

1. Cloud Management - Learn its Types, Benefits, Tools, Data-Flair (data-flair.training)
2. R. B. Uriarte, F. Tiezzi, R. De Nicola, SLAC: A Formal Service-Level-Agreement Language for Cloud Computing, IEEE/ACM 7th International Conference on Utility and Cloud Computing, London, Pages 419-426, 2014, DOI: 10.1109/UCC.2014.53.
3. T. Forell, D. Milojicic, V. Talwar, Cloud Management: Challenges and Opportunities, IEEE International Symposium on Parallel and Distributed Processing Workshops and Phd Forum, Shanghai, Pages 881-889,2011, DOI: 10.1109/IPDPS.2011.233.
4. E. B. Lakew, L. Xu, F. Hernández-Rodríguez, E. Elmroth, C. Pahl, A Synchronization Mechanism for Cloud Accounting Systems, International Conference on Cloud and Autonomic Computing, London, Pages 111-120, 2014, DOI: 10.1109/ICCAC.2014.11.
5. D. Talia, Clouds Meet Agents: Toward Intelligent Cloud Services, IEEE Internet Computing, Vol. 16, No. 2, Pages 78-81, 2012, DOI: 10.1109/MIC.2012.28.
6. The family of mapreduce and large-scale data processing systems, ACM Computing Surveys.

6

Cloud and Virtualization

Learning Objectives

- Understanding virtualization
- To give an insight of the characteristics in virtualization
- To learn the benefits associated with virtualization
- To give an insight of the techniques associated with virtualization

One of the underlying strides toward cloud computing is joining virtualization, which is isolating the equipment from the product. Before, advances of this size implied revamping code, for example, the progress from the centralized server to UNIX. Luckily, the progress to VMware doesn't require the change of code, and this has powered the speed of the push toward virtualization programming. There still will be difficulties in this change in any case, by and large; the combination of servers into the virtual world has been genuinely quick with numerous applications making a consistent progress. The adventure to get the chance to cloud computing starts with virtualization with the cloud OS giving framework and application administrations. The foundation administrations are the capacity to virtualize server, stockpiling, and the system, just as application benefits that give accessibility and security to the applications that are being used in the cloud condition. VMware's vSphere fulfils the underlying advance of virtualization, the division of the equipment and the product. The following stage is including a portion of the many cloud applications that incorporate how to do charge-backs and other application programming. These cloud-like capacities incorporate charging for use, the capacity to do self-administration, and numerous others. Charging for utilization, regardless of whether it is inside, will prompt better administration, with the capacity to monitor what administrations the buyer is using. Likewise, with cloud computing, there is simply the capacity to program in more help by the end client so as to minimize expenses.

Virtualization alludes to advancements intended to give a layer of deliberation between PC equipment frameworks and the product running on them. Virtualization intends to make a virtual variant of a gadget or asset, for example, a server, stockpiling gadget, organize or even a working framework where the structure separates the asset into at least one execution conditions. Indeed, even it is as straightforward as apportioning a hard drive is viewed as virtualization since you take one drive and parcel it to make two separate hard drives. Gadgets, applications and human clients can collaborate with the virtual asset as it were a genuine single sensible asset.

Cloud computing requires the utilization of virtualization, which is the division of the equipment and the product utilizing virtualization programming, for example, VMware's vSphere. Characterizing the various kinds of cloud computing furnishes us with information concerning what cloud computing brings to the table. Regardless of whether you are a purchaser or maker will characterize your meaning of cloud computing. The open cloud is truly intended more for the individual customer or little organization, while the private cloud is designed more for a medium-to huge organization. What's more, the private cloud is fanning out to join the capacity to have a few information and applications overhauled from the open cloud. Cloud computing depends intensely on virtualization. The administrations are based over a virtualization layers which help the specialist organizations to deal with the administration and offer institutionalized stage to the clients. Virtualization is in reality another key component of cloud computing, it empowers the specialist organization to offer the homogeneous help all the while to all clients, something that can't be accomplished, for instance, in lattice computing.

Major Components of Virtualization Environment

The goal of the virtualization is to make legitimate interface by abstracting the fundamental framework. Discussed below are some of the major components of virtualization:

Guest: Represents the segment that associates with the virtualization layer instead of with the host.
Host: This component helps in managing the guests.
Virtualization layer: This component manages calculation, capacity and system virtualization. Virtualized assets are exhibited in this layer.

Characteristics of Virtualization

With reference to Cloud Computing Environment, some significant qualities of virtualization are talked about as follows:

- **Association**: Through virtualization numerous OSs and different applications can keep running on the equivalent server. Both old and new forms of OS are equipped for conveying on the equivalent stage without extra venture on equipment.
- **Elasticity**: Application designer can run and test their applications in heterogeneous OS conditions utilizing same virtual machine. In virtualization condition, unique applications are segregated from one another in their separate virtual parcel.
- **Relocation and replication**: To progressively adjust the remaining task at hand, Virtual Machines are moved from one site to another. Because of which, clients can access refreshed equipment and make recuperation from equipment disappointment. Cloned virtual machines can be effectively sent on both nearby what's a more, remote destination.
- **Steadiness and security**: In virtualized condition, have OSs are fit for facilitating numerous guests OSs along with various applications. Each virtual machine is disengaged from other virtual machines and not in the least meddling into one another works which aides in accomplishing strength and security.
- **Para virtualization**: when the Guest OS can run on host OS with or without modification. In the event that any alteration is made to the working frameworks to be comfortable with Virtual Machine Manager, at that point this procedure is called as Para virtualization.

Importance of Virtualization in Cloud Computing

Virtualization in computing is production of virtual (not genuine) of virtual something, for example, equipment, programming, or a operating system or a storage or a network device. In a virtualized situation IT venture needs to oversee numerous progressions as the progressions happen more rapidly in virtual condition than in a physical domain.

- Cloud can exist without Virtualization, despite the fact that it

113

will be troublesome and wasteful.

- Cloud makes thought of Pay for what you use, boundless accessibility use as a lot of you need.
- Effective use of hardware resources is possible in cloud because of virtualization. By enabling a physical server to run virtualization programming, a server's assets are utilized significantly more effectively.
- At whatever point a business needs to extend its number of workstations or servers, Virtual machines can be an effective arrangement. There are no extra equipment costs, no requirement for extra physical space and no compelling reason to stick around. Virtual machine the board programming additionally makes it simpler for overseers to arrangement virtual machines and control access to specific assets, and so on.

Advantages of Virtualization in Cloud Computing

- **Economical**: Virtualization can decrease need of physical frameworks and you can get more an incentive out of the servers. Most generally constructed frameworks are underutilized. Virtualization permits most extreme utilization of the equipment speculation
- **Flexibility**: With virtualization, you can likewise run various kinds of uses and even run distinctive working frameworks for those applications on the equivalent physical equipment.
- **Security**: Using various virtual machines, it is conceivable to isolate benefits by running assistance on each virtual machine. This methodology is likewise called imprisoning of administrations.
- **Resource pooling**: It provides resource sharing, high utilization of pooled resources, rapid provisioning, and workload isolation. The recent trends in virtualization are consolidation of data centers thus reducing the managing cost.
- **Eliminates the risk of system failure**: During task implementation there are chances that the framework may crash down at an inappropriate time. This disappointment can make harm the organization however the virtualizations help you to play out a similar assignment in various gadgets simultaneously. The information can store in the cloud it can recover whenever and with the assistance of any gadget.

Drawbacks of Virtualization

- Managing virtual resources is basic and moving administrations of these resources are troublesome in accomplishing high accessibility.
- If one server fails, flat VM will be restarted on the other virtualized server in asset pool re-establishing the necessary administrations with least help interference.
- Virtual resources are basic for overseeing and information checking. Running applications with high usage and accessibility is a difficult issue.

Techniques of Virtualization

Virtual machine is computer software that runs operating system and applications. It is the duplication of real machine. The physical server on which one or more virtual machines are running is defined as host. The virtual machines are called guests. Multiple virtual systems (VMs) can run on a single physical system.

Guest OS Virtualization

In this situation the physical host PC framework runs a standard unmodified working framework, for example, Windows, Linux, Unix or MacOS. Running on this working framework is a virtualization application which executes similarly as some other application, for example, a word processor or spreadsheet would keep running on the framework. It is inside this virtualization application that at least one virtual machine are made to run the guest working frameworks on the host PC. The virtualization application is answerable for beginning, halting and dealing with each virtual machine and basically controlling access to physical equipment assets for the individual virtual machines. The virtualization application additionally takes part in a procedure known as parallel revamping which includes checking the guidance stream of the executing guest framework and supplanting any advantaged guidelines with safe copies. This has the impact of making the guest framework think it is running legitimately on the framework equipment, as opposed to in a virtual machine inside an application.

A few instances of guest OS virtualization innovations incorporate VMware Server and VirtualBox. The accompanying figure gives an outline of guest OS based virtualization:

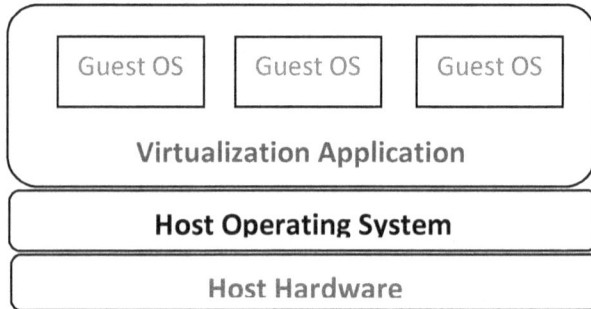

Figure 17. Guest OS virtualization.

As sketched out in the above outline, the guest working frameworks work in virtual machines inside the virtualization application which, thusly, keeps running over the host working framework similarly as some other application.

Operating System Virtualization

Operating system virtualization combines the features of LINUX and UNIX based frameworks. So as to see how Operating system virtualization functions it serves to initially comprehend the two fundamental segments of Linux or UNIX working frameworks. The kernel, in straightforward terms, handles every one of the connections between the working framework and the physical equipment. The second key part is the root document framework which contains every one of the libraries, records and utilities fundamental for the working framework to work. Under shared piece virtualization the virtual visitor frameworks each have their own root record framework yet share the bit of the host working framework. This structure is shown in the accompanying compositional outline:

This type of virtualization can able to alternate root document framework without rebooting the whole framework. Basically, shared part virtualization is an expansion of this ability. Maybe the greatest single downside of this type of virtualization is the way that the visitor working frameworks must be good with the variant of the piece which is being shared. It isn't, for instance, conceivable to run Microsoft Windows as a visitor on a Linux framework utilizing the common portion approach.

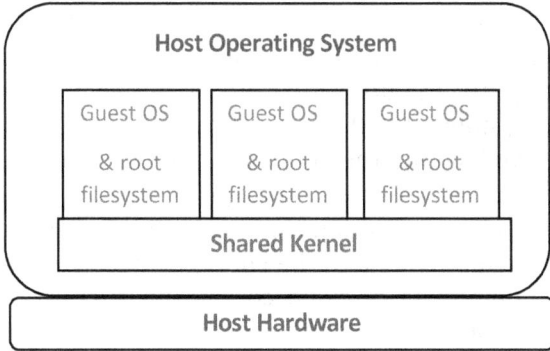

Figure 18. Operating system virtualization.

Linux VServer, Solaris Zones and Containers, FreeVPS and OpenVZ are all examples shared kernel virtualization solutions.

Kernel Level Virtualization

In this type of virtualization, the host OS keeps running on an exceptionally changed piece which contains expansions intended to oversee and control different virtual machines each containing a guest OS. Here each guest runs its own kernel, albeit comparative limitations apply in that the guest OS probably been arranged for a similar equipment as the bit in which they are running. Instances of part level virtualization advancements incorporate User Mode Linux (UML) and Kernel-based Virtual Machine (KVM). The accompanying outline gives a review of the piece level virtualization design:

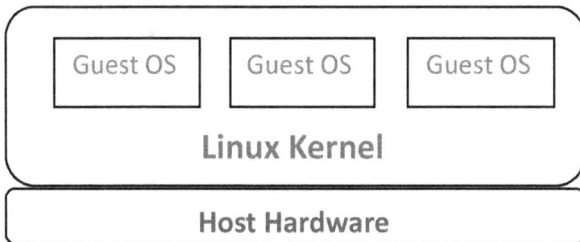

Figure 19. Kernel level virtualization.

Summary

This chapter provides a basic understanding of virtualization and its associated features along with techniques. Virtualization alludes to advancements intended to give a layer of deliberation between PC equipment frameworks and the product running on them. Cloud computing requires the utilization of virtualization, which is the division of the equipment and the product utilizing virtualization programming. Cloud computing depends intensely on virtualization. The administrations are based over a virtualization layers which help the specialist organizations to deal with the administration and offer institutionalized stage to the clients. Virtualization is in reality another key component of cloud computing, it empowers the specialist organization to offer the homogeneous help all the while to all clients, something that can't be accomplished, for instance, in lattice computing.

References

1. Cloud Computing Virtualization - Tutorialspoint
2. Virtualization in Cloud Computing - javatpoint
3. What is The Role of Virtualization in Cloud Computing, Techsolution

7

Cloud Security

Learning Objectives

- Understand the security aspects in cloud computing
- To give an insight about the security features in infrastructure
- Understanding privacy issues related to security
- Provide an insight regarding issues related to identity access management and access control

Public cloud computing requires a security model that directions adaptability and multi-tenure with the prerequisite for trust. Significant structure squares of trust and check connections incorporate access control, information security, consistence and occasion the board - all security components surely knew by IT offices today, actualized with existing items and advancements, and extendable into the cloud.

Not a single security technique will tackle these information insurances issues so it is imperative to think about numerous layers of resistance Security threats Organizations with characterized controls for remotely sourced administrations or access to IT hazard evaluation abilities should at present apply these parts of cloud administrations where suitable. However, while a considerable lot of the security risks of cloud cover with those of re-appropriating and offshoring, there are likewise contrasts that associations need to comprehend and oversee.

Preparing sensitive or business-basic information outside the venture presents a degree of hazard in light of the fact that any redistributed assistance sidesteps an association's in-house security controls. With cloud, be that as it may, it is conceivable to set up perfect controls if the supplier offers a hard work. An association ought to determine a supplier's situation by requesting data about the control and supervision of special overseers.

Associations utilizing cloud administrations stay answerable for the security and trustworthiness of their own information, in any event, when it is held by a specialist co-op. Customary specialist co-op are dependent upon outside reviews and security affirmations. Cloud suppliers may not be set up to experience a similar degree of investigation. At the point when an association utilizes a cloud administration, it may not know precisely where its information lives or have any capacity to impact changes to the area of information. Most suppliers store information in a common domain. In spite of the fact that this might be isolated from other clients' information while it's in that condition, it might be joined in reinforcement and chronicle duplicates.

Aspects of Cloud Security

- **Technology**: Associations embracing cloud administrations need to comprehend the suggestions for keeping up the classification of individual or other touchy business data. The key contemplations are the manner by which the physical or legitimate area of information influences its utilization and guaranteeing just determined clients and gadgets can see specific information. Purchasers need to comprehend the administrative systems under which they work, survey potential suppliers and attract up reasonable agreements to reflect administrative commitments. Everybody anticipates that specific data should be kept private in both their own and expert lives and they expect the associations for which they work, or with which they share their data, to keep up that confirmation of secrecy. On account of a completely overseen open cloud administration, protection and secrecy dangers are probably going to shift as per the supplier's terms of administration and security approach. There's a considerably more prominent degree of hazard where suppliers claim all authority to change their terms and approaches without plan of action for existing clients.
- **Data residency**: While considering public cloud services, instead of private or network clouds, an association needs to comprehend the potential hazard and effect of the auxiliary utilization of data. Optional utilization of certain data by the supplier may disregard the laws or terms under which that data was gathered. Given the difference in security enactment crosswise over various locales, the area where data is put away can affect the assurance of protection and secrecy just as

on the commitments of the individuals who procedure or store the data. Some administrative bodies and the laws of specific purviews build up protection benchmarks that can influence an association's choice to utilize a specific supplier especially where that supplier is offering an openly facilitated shared help. It is essential to comprehend the sorts of data put away and the fitting degree of hazard related with the loss of specific information.

- **Identify and classify**: In any case, while the area of information and the laws overseeing various wards are significant contemplations, it is likewise essential to comprehend the kinds of data put away and the suitable degree of hazard related with the loss of specific information. By recognizing and characterizing information, it is conceivable to think about the most proper area in which to store specific data. For instance, little information might be unreasonably delicate for an open cloud yet can in any case exist in a private one. For other information, advancements, for example, tokenisation could give the appropriate response. This is the place a delicate snippet of data is supplanted with a reference code and the real information is held in another database, facilitated somewhere else.

- **A joined-up approach**: The key thought for any association is to characterize a joint methodology among design, information the board, consistence and security groups, so as to distinguish the information that should be ensured, and the lawful and administrative commitments that relate to that information. Utilizing this blend of aptitudes and experience, an association can decide the suitable degree of assurance while as yet guaranteeing the information can be gotten to when and where important.

- **Legal or physical location**: It is imperative to comprehend the laws that may identify with the legitimate area of information (for example the area of the legitimate substance that holds the information, for example, the cloud supplier) instead of its physical area. Data in a cloud domain may have more than one legitimate area at any one time, with varying administrative ramifications. At times, a supplier may, without pulling out to its clients, move data from purview to locale, from supplier to supplier or from machine to machine.

- **Contract for confidentiality**: Where information residency is a significant issue, associations must ensure this is reflected in the legally binding game plans with their suppliers. It is critical to search for clear strategies and practices so as to settle on an educated choice about the protection and secrecy dangers. When drawing up cloud administration contracts, associations ought to consider adding information privacy provisions to guarantee suppliers don't make them rupture neighbourhood information enactment as a result of that suppliers' consistence with another ward's laws.

- **Access control**: The other key thought for guaranteeing the secrecy of cloud-based information is getting to control. Cloud-facilitated information can be gotten to through a larger number of directs and in a bigger number of areas than information facilitated in the association. With a potential large number of gadgets and remote clients looking for access from changed worldwide areas, by means of a blend of open and private Wi-Fi, versatile systems and fixed associations, it is crucial associations guarantee classified data isn't undermined and that their entrance control strategies are as yet supported by their utilization of cloud administrations.

- **The challenge of multiple logins**: Having numerous logins for various administrations is probably going to lessen get to security. This is on the grounds that it makes clients bound to store passwords unreliably on their gadgets or paper as opposed to submitting them to memory. Along these lines, when characterizing access control systems for cloud applications and information, associations should attempt to guarantee their methodology is coordinated with their in-house models. Numerous associations are utilizing single sign-on (SSO) to lighten the security issues displayed by various logins. This can result in included multifaceted nature where there are various cloud suppliers notwithstanding inward administrations. Associations ought to find out whether it is fitting to join forces with at least one confided in personality suppliers, SSO can proceed. The entrance control model ought to likewise explain who decides the trusted and confiding in gatherings, and how.

- **Granular data control**: Various pieces of the business by and large just expect access to a specific subset of the association's information. For instance, it's improbable that retail staff would need to get to their association's legitimate and business applications. It might in this way merit considering job-based access control to additionally lessen the danger of secret data falling into an inappropriate hand. In fact, it will be progressively alluring to control access to information at a considerably more granular level.

Infrastructure Security

IaaS Security Storage equipment or servers can be physically gotten to and traded off. This can prompt disavowal of administration assault and, contingent upon the idea of the assault, this could prompt loss of significant information accessibility. Classification could be an issue if the assailant can see information at a server farm an issue that is taken care of by utilization of encryption and access controls; however aggressors can generally discover their way around these obstructions. Cloud programming can have bugs and vulnerabilities that can be misused. Virtual machines are portable and the hypervisor stores the virtual machines as records, making the virtual machines helpless against duplicating to another gadget. The capacity of an assailant to duplicate a virtual machine gives the aggressor the benefit of attempting to break into the framework without recognition since these assaults are being performed on a duplicate of the virtual machine.

IaaS application suppliers treat the applications inside the client virtual occurrence as a black box and along these lines are totally not interested in the tasks and the board of a uses of the client.

Infrastructure Security: The Network Level

When considering at the system level of infrastructure security, it is critical to recognize open clouds and private clouds. With private clouds, there are no new assaults, vulnerabilities, or changes in hazard explicit to this topology that data security work force need to consider. In spite of the fact that your association's IT design may change with the execution of a private cloud, your present system topology will presumably not change fundamentally. On the off chance that you have a private extranet set up, for down to earth purposes you most likely have the system topology for a private cloud set up as of now. The security contemplations you have today apply to a private cloud framework, as well. What's more, the security instruments you have set up are likewise important for a private cloud and work similarly.

Be that as it may, on the off chance that you decide to utilize open cloud administrations, changing security necessities will expect changes to your system topology. You should address how your current system topology cooperates with your cloud supplier's system topology. There are four huge hazard factors in this utilization case:

- Ensuring the privacy and trustworthiness of your association's information in-travel to and from your open cloud supplier.
- Ensuring legitimate access control (confirmation, approval, and inspecting) to whatever assets you are utilizing at your open cloud supplier.
- Ensuring the accessibility of the internet-confronting assets in an open cloud that are being utilized by your association, or have been allocated to your association by your open cloud suppliers.
- Replacing the set-up model of system zones and levels with areas.

Infrastructure Security: The Host Level

When exploring hosts security and evaluating dangers, you ought to consider the setting of cloud administrations conveyance models (SaaS, PaaS, and IaaS) and organization models (public, private, and hybrid). In spite of the fact that there are no known new dangers to have that are explicit to cloud figuring, some virtualization security dangers, for example, VM escape, framework arrangement float, and insider dangers by method for frail access control to the hypervisor convey into the general population cloud processing condition. The dynamic nature (flexibility) of cloud processing can bring new operational difficulties from a security the board point of view. The operational model propels fast provisioning and short lived occurrences of VMs. Overseeing vulnerabilities and patches is thusly a lot harder than simply running an output, as the pace of progress is a lot higher than in a conventional server farm. Likewise, the way that the clouds tackle the intensity of thousands of register hubs, joined with the homogeneity of the working framework utilized by has, implies the dangers can be enhanced rapidly and effectively consider it the "speed of assault" factor in the cloud. All the more critically, you ought to comprehend the trust limit and the duties that fall on your shoulders to verify the host foundation that you oversee. Also, you should contrast the equivalent and suppliers' obligations in verifying the piece of the host framework the CSP oversees.

SaaS and PaaS Host Security

In general, CSPs don't freely share data identified with their host stages, have working frameworks, and the procedures that are set up to verify the hosts, since programmers can misuse that data when they are attempting to encroach into the cloud administration. Thus, in the setting of SaaS (e.g., Salesforce.com, Workday.com) or PaaS (e.g., Google App Engine) cloud administrations, have security is murky to clients and the obligation of verifying the hosts is consigned to the CSP. To get affirmation from the CSP on the security cleanliness of its hosts, you ought to request that the seller share data under a nondisclosure agreement (NDA) or just request that the CSP share the data by means of a controls appraisal structure, for example, SysTrust or ISO 27002. From a controls confirmation point of view, the CSP needs to guarantee that proper preventive and analyst controls are in place and should guarantee the equivalent by means of an outsider appraisal or ISO 27002 sort evaluation structure. Since virtualization is a key empowering innovation that improves have equipment use, among different advantages, it is basic for CSPs to utilize virtualization stages, including Xen also, VMware hypervisors, in their host processing stage design. You ought to see how the supplier is utilizing virtualization innovation and the supplier's procedure for verifying the virtualization layer. Both the PaaS and SaaS stages theoretical and conceal the host working framework from end clients with a host deliberation layer. One key contrast among PaaS and SaaS is the openness of the deliberation layer that shrouds the working framework benefits the applications devour. In the instance of SaaS, the deliberation layer isn't noticeable to clients and is accessible just to the engineers what's more, the CSP's tasks staff, where PaaS clients are given backhanded access to host deliberation layer as a PaaS application programming interface (API) that associates with host reflection layer. So, on the off chance that you are a SaaS or a PaaS client, you are depending on the CSP to give a protected host stage on which the SaaS or PaaS application is created also, conveyed by the CSP and you, individually.

Infrastructure Security: The Application Level

Application or programming security ought to be a basic component of your security program. Most ventures with data security programs still can't seem to establish an application security program to address this domain. Structuring and executing applications focused for arrangement on a cloud stage will necessitate that current application security programs rethink current practices and models. The application security range ranges from independent single-client applications to advanced multiuser online business applications utilized by a large number of clients. Web applications, for example, content administration frameworks (CMSs), wikis, entries, notice sheets, and talk discussions are utilized by little and enormous associations. A huge number of associations likewise create and keep up exclusively fabricated web applications for their organizations utilizing different web structures (PHP, .NET, J2EE, Ruby on Rails, Python, and so on.). As per SANS, until 2007 not many crooks assaulted helpless sites on the grounds that other assault vectors were bound to prompt a bit of leeway in unapproved monetary or data get to. Progressively, in any case, propels in cross-site scripting (XSS) and other assaults have shown that hoodlums searching for monetary profit can abuse vulnerabilities coming about because of web programming mistakes as better approaches to enter significant associations. In this area, we will confine our discourse to web application security: web applications in the cloud got to by clients with standard Internet programs, for example, Firefox, Internet Explorer, or Safari, from any PC associated with the Internet. Since the program has developed as the end client customer for getting to in-cloud applications, it is significant for application security projects to incorporate program security into the extent of application security. Together they decide the quality of start to finish cloud security that ensures the secrecy, honesty, and accessibility of the data handled by cloud administrations.

Application-Level Security Threats

Equipped with information and devices, programmers are always checking web applications for application vulnerabilities. They are then misusing the vulnerabilities they find for different criminal operations including money related extortion, licensed innovation burglary, changing over believed sites into vindictive servers serving customer side adventures, and phishing tricks. All web structures and a wide range of web applications are in danger of web application security deserts, extending from inadequate approval to application rationale mistakes. It has been a typical practice to utilize a blend of edge security controls and system and host-based access controls to secure web applications sent in a firmly controlled condition, including corporate intranets and private clouds, from outer programmers. Web applications assembled and conveyed in an open cloud stage will be exposed to a high danger level, assaulted, and possibly abused by programmers to help fake and criminal operations.

SaaS Application Security

The SaaS model directs that the supplier deals with the whole suite of utilizations conveyed to clients. Hence, SaaS suppliers are to a great extent liable for verifying the applications and segments they offer to clients. Clients are normally liable for operational security capacities, including client and access the board as upheld by the supplier. It is a typical practice for imminent clients, normally under a NDA, to demand data identified with the supplier's security rehearses. This data ought to incorporate structure, engineering, improvement, highly contrasting box application security testing, and discharge the board. A few clients go to the degree of contracting autonomous security merchants to perform entrance testing of SaaS applications to pick up affirmation freely. Be that as it may, infiltration testing can be expensive and not all suppliers consent to this kind of confirmation. Additional consideration should be paid to the verification and access control highlights offered by SaaS CSPs. Normally that is the main security control accessible to oversee hazard to data. Most administrations, including those from Salesforce.com and Google, offer an online organization UI device to oversee confirmation and access control of the application. Some SaaS applications, for example, Google Apps, have worked in highlights that end clients can summon to relegate peruse and compose benefits to different clients. In any case, the benefit the executives highlight may not be propelled, fine-grained get to and could have shortcomings that may not fit in with your association's entrance control standard. One model that catches this issue is the instrument that Google Docs utilizes in taking care of pictures inserted in archives, just as access benefits to more established variants of a record. Clearly, implanted pictures put away in Google Docs are not ensured similarly that a report is secured with sharing controls. That implies on the off chance that you have shared a report containing installed pictures, the other individual will consistently have the option to see those pictures considerably after you've halted sharing the report. A blogger‖ found this entrance control characteristic and carried it to Google's consideration. Despite the fact that Google has recognized the issue, its reaction passes on that it believes those worries don't represent a huge security hazard to its clients.

PaaS Application Security

PaaS merchants comprehensively fall into the accompanying two significant classifications:

- Software merchants (e.g., Bungee, Etelos, GigaSpaces, Eucalyptus)
- CSPs (e.g., Google App Engine, Salesforce.com, Microsoft Azure, Intuit QuickBase)

Associations assessing a private cloud may use PaaS programming to assemble an answer for inward utilization. Right now, no significant open clouds are known to utilize business off-the-rack or open source PaaS programming, for example, (Eucalyptus offers a restricted test pilot cloud for designers at Eucalyptus.com, be that as it may). In this way, given the early phase of PaaS arrangement, we won't talk about programming security of independent PaaS programming in this part. In any case, it is suggested that associations assessing PaaS programming play out a hazard appraisal and apply the product security standard like gaining any endeavour programming. By definition, a PaaS cloud (open or private) offers an incorporated domain to plan, create, test, send, and bolster custom applications created in the language the stage bolsters. PaaS application security incorporates two programming layers:

- Security of the PaaS stage itself (i.e., runtime motor)
- Security of client applications conveyed on a PaaS stage

As a rule, PaaS CSPs (e.g., Google, Microsoft, and Force.com) are liable for verifying the stage programming stack that incorporates the runtime motor that runs the client applications. Since PaaS applications may utilize outsider applications, segments, or web administrations, the outsider application supplier might be liable for verifying their administrations. Subsequently, clients ought to comprehend the reliance of their application on all administrations and survey dangers relating to outsider specialist co-ops. As of not long ago, CSPs have been hesitant to share data relating to stage security utilizing the contention that such security data could give a bit of leeway to programmers. Be that as it may, undertaking clients ought to request straightforwardness from CSPs and look for data important to perform chance evaluation also, continuous security the board.

Data Security and Storage

Concerning data in transit, the essential hazard is in not utilizing a reviewed encryption calculation. In spite of the fact that this is evident to data security experts, rarely for others to comprehend this prerequisite when utilizing an open cloud, paying little mind to whether it is IaaS, PaaS, or on the other hand SaaS. It is additionally essential to guarantee that a convention gives classification just as uprightness (e.g., FTP over SSL [FTPS], Hypertext Transfer Protocol Secure [HTTPS], and Secure Copy Program [SCP]) especially if the convention is utilized for moving information over the Internet. Only scrambling information and utilizing a non-verified convention (e.g., vanilla or straight FTP or HTTP) can give secrecy, yet doesn't guarantee the honesty of the information (e.g., with the utilization of symmetric spilling figures). In spite of the fact that utilizing encryption to secure information very still may appear glaringly evident, the fact of the matter isn't that straightforward. In the event that you are utilizing an IaaS cloud administration (public or private) for basic storage (e.g., Amazon's Simple Storage Service or S3), encoding information very still is conceivable and is unequivocally proposed. Nonetheless, encoding information very still that a PaaS or SaaS cloud-based application is utilizing (e.g., Google Apps, Salesforce.com) as a repaying control isn't constantly achievable. Information very still utilized by a cloud-based application is for the most part not scrambled, on the grounds that encryption would anticipate ordering or looking of that information. By and large talking, with information very still, the financial matters of cloud registering are to such an extent that PaaS based applications and SaaS utilize a multitenancy engineering. As it were, information, when prepared by a cloud-based application or put away for use by a cloud-based application, is coexisted with other clients' information (i.e., it is ordinarily put away in a huge information store, for example, Google's BigTable). Despite the fact that applications are regularly planned with highlights, for example, information labelling to avert unapproved access to mixed together information, unapproved get to is as yet conceivable through some adventure of an application helplessness (e.g., Google's unapproved information sharing between clients of Records and Spreadsheets in March 2009). Albeit some cloud suppliers have their applications looked into by outsiders or checked with outsider application security devices, information isn't on a stage devoted exclusively to one association. Albeit an association's information in-travel may be scrambled during move to and from a cloud supplier, and its information very still may be scrambled if utilizing straightforward storage (i.e., on the off chance that it isn't related with a detail application), an association's information is certainly not scrambled on the off chance that it is handled in the cloud. For any application to process information, that information must be decoded. Until June 2009, there was no known strategy for completely handling scrambled information. In this way, except if the information is in the cloud for just basic storage, the information will be decoded during in any event part of its life cycle in the cloud preparing at the very least.

Data Security Mitigation

In the event that planned clients of cloud processing administrations expect that information security will fill in as repaying controls for conceivably debilitated framework security, since part of a client's framework security moves outside its ability to control and a supplier's infrastructure security may (for some ventures) or may not (for little to medium-size organizations, or SMBs) be less strong than desires, you will be disillusioned. In spite of the fact that information in-travel can and ought to be encoded, any utilization of that information in the cloud, past straightforward storage, necessitates that it be decoded. In this manner, it is practically sure that in the cloud, information will be decoded. Furthermore, on the off chance that you are utilizing a PaaS-based application or SaaS, client decoded information will likewise very likely be facilitated in a multitenancy domain (in public clouds). Add to that presentation even numerous suppliers' inability to satisfactorily address such a fundamental security worry as information permanence, and the dangers of information security for clients are essentially expanded. Things being what they are, what would it be a good idea for you to do to alleviate these dangers to information security? The main suitable choice for relief is to guarantee that any touchy or directed information isn't set into a public cloud (or that you encode information put into the cloud for basic storage as it were). Given the financial contemplations of cloud figuring today, just as the present furthest reaches of cryptography, CSPs are not offering powerful enough controls around information security. It might be that those financial matters change and that suppliers offer their present administrations, just as an administrative cloud condition (i.e., a domain where clients are eager to pay more for upgraded security controls to appropriately deal with delicate and directed information). Right now, the main suitable alternative for alleviation is to guarantee that any delicate or managed information isn't placed into a public cloud.

Storage

For data stored in the cloud (i.e., storage-as-a-service), we are referring to IaaS and not data associated with an application running in the cloud on PaaS or SaaS. The same three information security concerns are associated with this data stored in the cloud (e.g., Amazon's S3) as with data stored elsewhere: confidentiality, integrity, and availability.

Confidentiality

When it comes to the confidentiality of data stored in a public cloud, you have two potential concerns:

- Firstly, what access control exists to secure the information? Access control comprises of both confirmation and approval. CSPs for the most part utilize weak authentication mechanisms (e.g., username + secret phrase/password), and the approval (get to) controls accessible to clients will in general be very coarse and not extremely granular. For enormous associations, this coarse approval presents huge security concerns unto itself. Frequently, the main approval levels cloud merchants give are chairman approval (i.e., the proprietor of the record itself) and client approval (i.e., all other approved clients) without any levels in the middle of (e.g., specialty unit managers, who are approved to affirm access for their own specialty unit work force). Once more, these entrance control issues are not one of a kind to CSPs.

- The second potential concern: how is the information that is put away in the cloud really ensured? For every single viable reason, insurance of information put away in the cloud includes the utilization of encryption. Things being what they are, is a client's information really encoded when it is put away in the cloud? What's more, provided that this is true, with what encryption calculation, and with what key quality? It depends, and explicitly, it relies upon which CSP you are utilizing.

- The next thought for you is the thing that key length is utilized. With symmetric encryption, the more drawn out the key length (i.e., the more noteworthy number of bits in the key), the more grounded the encryption. Albeit long key lengths give more assurance, they are likewise more computationally lengths ought to be at least 112 bits for Triple DES (Data Encryption Standard) and 128-bits for AES (Advanced Encryption Standard) both NIST-endorsed calculations.

- Another secrecy thought for encryption is key administration. How are the encryption keys that are utilized going to be overseen and by whom? It is safe to say that you will deal with your own keys? Ideally, the appropriate response is truly, and ideally you have the skill to deal with your own keys. It isn't prescribed that you depend a cloud supplier to deal with your keys at any rate not a similar supplier that is taking care of your information. This implies extra assets and abilities are fundamental. That being stated, legitimate key administration is a mind boggling and troublesome errand. Since key administration is unpredictable and hard for a solitary client, it is much increasingly intricate and hard for CSPs to attempt to appropriately deal with numerous clients' keys. Therefore, a few CSPs don't work admirably of dealing with clients' keys. For instance, it is regular for a supplier to encode the entirety of a client's information with a solitary key. Far and away more terrible, we know about one cloud storage supplier that utilizes a solitary encryption key for the entirety of its clients.

Integrity

Notwithstanding the confidentiality of your information, you additionally need to stress over the honesty of your information. Secrecy doesn't infer trustworthiness; information can be scrambled for privacy purposes, but then you probably won't have an approach to check the respectability of that information. Encryption alone is adequate for privacy; however, trustworthiness likewise requires the utilization of message authentication codes (MACs). The least complex approach to utilize MACs on encoded information is to utilize a square symmetric calculation (rather than a gushing symmetric calculation cipher block chaining (CBC) mode and to incorporate a one-way hash function. This isn't for the cryptographically unenlightened and it is one motivation behind why compelling key administration is troublesome.

In any event, cloud clients ought to get some information about these issues. Not exclusively is this significant for the respectability of a client's information, however it will likewise serve to give knowledge on how complex a supplier's security program is or isn't. Keep in mind, notwithstanding, that not all suppliers scramble client information, particularly for PaaS and SaaS administrations. Another part of information uprightness is significant, particularly with mass stockpiling utilizing IaaS. When a client has a few gigabytes (or a greater amount of) its information up in the cloud for capacity, how does the client keep an eye on the uprightness of the information put away there? There are IaaS move costs related with moving information into and withdraw from the cloud, just as system usage (data transmission) contemplations for the client's own system. What a client truly needs to do is to approve the honesty of its information while that information stays in the cloud without downloading and reupload that information. This errand is much progressively troublesome in light of the fact that it must be done in the cloud without express information overall informational index. Clients by and large don't know on which physical machines their information is put away, or where those frameworks are found. Also, that informational collection is presumably powerful and evolving much of the time. Those regular changes hinder the viability of customary uprightness protection systems. What is required rather is a proof of retrievability that is, a numerical method to check the honesty of information as it is progressively put away in the cloud.

Availability

Accepting that a client's information has kept up its privacy and respectability, you should likewise be worried about the accessibility of your information. There are at present three significant dangers in this respect none of which are new to registering, however all of which take on expanded significance in cloud registering on account of expanded hazard. The primary danger to accessibility is network-based attacks, followed by danger to CSP's own accessibility.

Data Security and Privacy Issues

Information Breaches

At the point when client utilizes administrations of cloud processing, they may require some secret data like charge card data at the point when ordinary handling is occurs by then of time it might conceivable that some unapproved client may burglary the private data and they can abuse the data. Consequently, there is danger of information break in cloud processing.

Information Loss

An information rupture is the consequence of a vindictive and presumably meddlesome activity. Information misfortune may emerge when plate drive kicks the bucket without proprietor of information had not made reinforcement. Furthermore, here and there it additionally may happen that, there was scrambled information which is bolted and some key are important to open the information and around then information get misfortune when the key get misfortune. Information misfortune likewise done by the human and they may do this sort of thing for purposefully.

Record or Service Traffic Hijacking

There are numerous administrations on web however for utilizing they client need to make their record and afterward they can begin utilizing the administrations. Record capturing is normal factor in cloud. Now and then because of programming vulnerabilities, dealing and support flood it might happen. This all hazard may prompt loss of command over their record. A criminal oversee client record can listen in on exchange, control information, give bogus reactions to clients.

Insecure APIs

The cloud time has achieved the inconsistency of attempting to make administrations accessible to millions while restricting any harm all these generally mysterious clients may do to the administration. The appropriate response has been a public confronting application programming interface, or API, that characterizes how an outsider associates an application to the administration and giving check that the outsider creating the application is who he says he is Leading web engineers, including ones from Twitter and Google, teamed up on indicating OAuth, an open approval administration for web benefits that controls outsider access.

There are unpredictable information security challenges in the cloud:

- The need to ensure classified business, government, or administrative information
- Cloud administration models with numerous inhabitants having a similar foundation
- Data versatility and lawful issues comparative with such government rules
- Lack of norms about how cloud specialist co-ops safely reuse circle space and delete existing information
- Auditing, revealing, and consistence concerns
- Loss of perceivability to key security and operational knowledge that never again is accessible to take care of big business IT security insight and hazard the board

It is important to beat this wide range of hazard. It is requiring utilizing the security controls that ensure touchy and assists with defeating information misfortune, information break and record dealing. There are some viable cloud security arrangement should consolidate three key capacities:

- First, ensure that information isn't coherent and that the arrangement offers solid key administration.

- Second, actualize get to strategies that guarantee just approved clients can access touchy data, so that even advantaged clients, for example, root client can't see delicate data.
- Third, consolidate security insight that produces log data, which can be utilized for conduct examination to give alarms that trigger when clients are performing activities outside of the standard.

Information Ownership

The association's proprietorship rights over the information must be solidly settled in the administration agreement to empower a reason for trust. The proceeding with contention over security and information proprietorship rights for long range interpersonal communication clients outlines the effect that uncertain terms can host on the gatherings in question. In a perfect world, the agreement should state obviously that the association holds responsibility for its information; that the cloud supplier procures no rights or licenses through the consent to utilize the information for its own motivations, including protected innovation rights or licenses; and that the cloud supplier doesn't gain and may not guarantee any security enthusiasm for the information. For these arrangements to fill in as proposed, the terms of information proprietorship must not be dependent upon one-sided correction by the cloud supplier.

Information Location

One of the most widely recognized consistence issues confronting an association is information area. Utilization of an in-house registering focus permits an association to structure its processing condition and to know in detail where information is put away and what shields are utilized to secure the information. Interestingly, a quality of many cloud figuring administrations is that point by point data about the area of an association's information is inaccessible or not uncovered to the administration endorser. This circumstance makes it hard to find out whether adequate shields are set up and whether legitimate and administrative consistence prerequisites are met.

Jurisdictional Issues

To comprehend the security and lawful insurances accessible inside the domain of cloud processing, one must address the issue of ward. Since clients can get to their data from for all intents and purposes any area with an Internet association, it is hazy where the information is really being put away. For instance, on the off chance that somebody gets to cloud data put away on a server in Europe from his home in the United States, which laws and guidelines apply? There are various geographical contemplations to consider while tending to lawful and security worries in the cloud. In their article examining jurisdictional issues in cloud registering, various researchers depict the central factors in server and server farm area. As per the researchers, four essential contemplations must be considered by cloud suppliers in picking where to develop a server farm:

- appropriate physical space in which to develop the stockroom measured structures;
- vicinity to high-limit Internet associations;
- the plenitude of moderate power and other vitality assets; and
- the laws, strategies, and guideline of the locale.

The area of a cloud supplier's server farm enormously influences the manner by which clients are legitimately secured. It is misty where a case will be attempted when a cloud supplier is included. Singular wards differ as far as cloud arrangement and guideline. Server farms situated in the United States are helpless against "insight gathering instruments like the USA PATRIOT Act, the Homeland Security Act, and the National Security Letters." Many approach issues become an integral factor in various regions and impacts affect suppliers. It is especially essential to take note of that these arrangements propel a cloud supplier "to agree to a subpoena for a client's data without informing the client concerning the subpoena." To stay away from the scope of these laws, suppliers have started development of server farms in areas that are not dependent upon them. A worldwide financial association, known as SWIFT, is thinking about an unbiased nation (Switzerland) as its server farm, trying to maintain a strategic distance from lawful intricacies and dangers. Legitimate issues raised by cloud registering, particularly those including locale, have to a great extent stayed unaddressed.

Challenges and Legal Issues involved in Cloud Computing

Each new innovation carries bunches of points of interest alongside it, and cloud registering isn't a special case to it. Anyway it has some hazy areas additionally which should be replied. The wide utilization of cloud processing in the course of recent years has raised a few issues. It must be comprehend that the motivation behind cloud registering administration is to encourage the processing needs of hundreds and thousands associations over a virtual figuring foundation found some place on the Internet, which is particularly opposing to the regular specialist co-ops. Along these lines it gets significant with respect to the associations to get affirmation that their information will be sheltered, and secure.

Besides, there are some specialized and legitimate issues, as:

- **Information privacy and confidentiality**: Data protection and classification are two significant issues with cloud processing. Cloud office can be profited by any individual or association. It might happen that a person who is utilizing cloud office wouldn't free offering his information to cloud specialist organization; however the equivalent may not be the situation with the establishments or organizations. There are reasonable possibilities that a few associations or organizations might be modest in offering their data to cloud specialist co-op. There are chances that a few organizations may have their own laws that limit the sharing of their information completely. In such cases it gets significant for all the gatherings associated with cloud registering to be very much aware about the laws which might be impossible from the client's perspective. Where data is of delicate nature, for example, guard, aviation, business and so forth it is profoundly necessitated that such information is very much defended.
- Reinforcement backup of the significant information has consistently been a significant concern. Presently if an association that is profiting cloud office takes the reinforcement of the information on its own current server then the very motivation behind moving the information to a cloud would be crushed. On the opposite end, in the event that the reinforcement is assumed to have a control over the cloud, the issues of information protection and security will still remain.

- **Capture attempt of information**: There are a few nations that have laws relating to block attempt of information. During the pendency of suits, it might be compulsory for an organization to offer access to the information to the exploring office. In such cases, since the information is situated in cloud, it might get hard for the office to approach such information.
- **Go-between**: The fundamental motivation behind the middle people in the virtual world is to encourage the changes between outsider on the web. Delegates in the virtual world unite or encourage exchanges between outsiders on the web. These delegates give virtual access to have, and transmit items/administrations started by outsiders. Practically under all information security laws there are sure guidelines by ethicalness of which these go-betweens are pardoned of liabilities. In such cases the associations that benefit cloud registering administrations must to check that their privileges are successfully ensured under the laws.
- Information storage location regarding where the information must be put away it must be a client who ought to have that decision. If there should arise an occurrence of cloud registering the subtleties with respect to where the information is put away isn't known to the associations. Once more, there could be different clouds moreover. This may influence the security laws of one purview that is burdensome then the other ward. In such cases it becomes significant fix the risk regarding who can be considered dependable if there should be an occurrence of information is lost.
- **Overseeing laws and jurisdiction**: According to the conventional regrets of private universal law, the purview of a country just stretches out to people who are inside the nation or to the exchanges and occasions that happen inside the common fringes of the country. In any case, these conventional principles relating to purview has gotten less compelling with the progression of business and innovation. In instances of cloud exchanges, it might happen that an organization which is occupant of one nation may put away information on a cloud which is situated in out and out various nation and such cloud may have a place with a merchant who is situated in a third nation. In such cases there are adequate possibilities that the laws of third wards are pertinent.

Identity and Access Management

In the present cloud registering world, it turns out to be very muddle to shield information from unapproved. Personality the board center around who is proprietor of information which gives that specific data is of this specific proprietor. Identity principally center on protection of client data. Though get to the executives primarily center around an openness of data. Access Management worry about who have the consent to get to information.

Information affectability and protection of data has become progressively a zone of worry for associations and unapproved access to data assets in the cloud is a significant concern. One repeating issue is that the authoritative recognizable proof and verification structure may not normally stretch out into the cloud and broadening or changing the current system to help cloud administrations might be troublesome The option of utilizing two diverse validation frameworks, one for the inside hierarchical frameworks and another for outer cloud-based frameworks, is a confusion that can get unworkable after some time. Identity federation, promoted with the presentation of administration arranged structures, is one arrangement that can be practiced in various manners, for example, with the Security Assertion Markup Language (SAML) standard or the OpenID standard.

Authentication is the way toward checking the identity of a client or framework (e.g., Lightweight Catalog Access Protocol [LDAP] confirming the qualifications exhibited by the client, where the identifier is the corporate client ID that is special and doled out to a worker or contractual worker). Verification for the most part implies a progressively strong type of recognizable proof. In a few use cases, for example, administration to-support cooperation, validation includes checking the organize administration mentioning access to data served by another help (e.g., a movement web administration that is associating with a Visa door to confirm the charge card for benefit of the client).

Authorization is the way toward deciding the benefits the client or framework is qualified for when the identity is built up. With regards to computerized administrations, approval as a rule follows the validation step and is utilized to decide if the client or administration has the fundamental benefits to play out specific tasks—at the end of the day, approval is the way toward authorizing arrangements.

Auditing with regards to IAM, inspecting involves the procedure of survey and assessment of verification, approval records, and exercises to decide the ampleness of IAM framework controls, to confirm consistence with set up security arrangements and techniques (e.g., partition of obligations), to recognize breaks in security administration's (e.g., benefit heightening), and to suggest any progressions that are shown for countermeasures.

IAM Challenges

One basic test of IAM concerns overseeing access for different client populaces (representatives, temporary workers, accomplices, and so on.) getting to inner and remotely facilitated administrations. IT is continually tested to quickly arrangement fitting access to the clients whose jobs and duties regularly change for business reasons. Another issue is the turnover of clients inside the association. Turnover shifts by industry and capacity occasional staffing variances in account offices, for instance and can likewise emerge from changes in the business, for example, mergers and acquisitions, new item and administration discharges, business process re-appropriating, and evolving duties. Therefore, continuing IAM procedures can transform into a determined challenge.

Access arrangements for data are only from time to time halfway and reliably applied. Associations can contain divergent indexes, making complex snare of client personalities, get to rights, and techniques. This has prompted wasteful aspects in client and accesses the executive's forms while presenting these associations to critical security, administrative consistence, and Reputation dangers.

To address these difficulties and dangers, numerous organizations have looked for innovation answers for empower incorporated and robotized client get to the executives. A large number of these activities are gone into with exclusive standards, which isn't astounding given that the issue is regularly enormous and complex. Regularly those activities to improve IAM can traverse quite a long while and bring about impressive expense. Consequently, associations should move toward their IAM methodology and design with both business and IT drivers that address the center wastefulness issues while safeguarding the control's adequacy (identified with get to control). At exactly that point will the associations have a higher probability of progress and rate of profitability.

IAM Architecture and Practice

IAM is anything but a solid arrangement that can be handily conveyed to pick up capacities right away. It is as a lot of a part of design as it is an assortment of innovation segments, procedures, and standard practices. Standard venture IAM engineering incorporates a few layers of innovation, administrations, and procedures. At the center of the arrangement engineering is an index administration, (for example, LDAP or Active Directory) that goes about as an archive for the identity, qualification, and client traits of the association's client pool. The registry cooperates with IAM innovation segments, for example, validation, client the executives, provisioning, and alliance benefits that help the standard IAM practice and procedures inside the association. The IAM procedures to help the business can be comprehensively sorted as follows:

- User management activities for the compelling administration and the board of identity life cycles.
- Authentication management activities for the compelling administration and the executives of the procedure for verifying that a substance is who or what it professes to be.
- Authorization management activities for the powerful administration and the board of the procedure for deciding privilege rights that choose what assets a substance is allowed to access as per the association's arrangements.
- Access management enforcement of approaches for get to control in light of a solicitation from a substance needing to get to an IT asset inside the association.
- Data management and provisioning propagation of identity and information for approval to IT assets by means of computerized or manual procedures.
- Monitoring, auditing, reviewing, and revealing consistence by clients in regards to access to assets inside the association dependent on the characterized approaches.

IAM processes support the following operational activities:

- **Provisioning**
  This is the procedure of on-boarding clients to frameworks and applications. These procedures give clients essential access to information and innovation assets. The term regularly is utilized in reference to big business level asset the executives. Provisioning can be thought of as a blend of the obligations of the HR and IT divisions, where clients are offered access to information archives or frameworks, applications, and databases dependent on a interesting client identity. Deprovisioning works in the contrary way coming about in the erasure or deactivation of an identity or of benefits appointed to the client identity.

- **Credential and attribute management**
  Accreditation and property the board These procedures are intended to deal with the existence pattern of accreditations and client characteristics make, issue, oversee, deny to limit the business hazard related with identity pantomime and unseemly record use. Accreditations are normally bound to an individual and are confirmed during the validation procedure. The procedures incorporate provisioning of traits, static (e.g., standard content secret key) and dynamic (e.g., once secret word) qualifications that agree to a secret word standard (e.g., passwords impervious to lexicon assaults), taking care of secret word termination, encryption the board of qualifications during travel and very still, and access approaches of client characteristics (protection and treatment of properties for different administrative reasons).

- **Entitlement management**
  Privileges are likewise alluded to as approval arrangements. The procedures right now address the provisioning and deprovisioning of benefits required for the client to get to assets including frameworks, applications, and databases. Legitimate privilege the board guarantees that clients are allocated just the necessary benefits (least benefits) that coordinate with their activity capacities. Privilege the board can be utilized to fortify the security of web administrations, web applications, inheritance applications, records and documents, and physical security frameworks.

- **Compliance management**
  This procedure infers that entrance rights and benefits are checked and followed to guarantee the security of an undertaking's assets. The procedure additionally assists evaluators with checking consistence to different interior access control arrangements, and guidelines that incorporate practices, for example, isolation of obligations, get to observing, intermittent evaluating, and announcing. A model is a client accreditation process that permits application proprietors to ensure that solitary approved clients have the benefits important to get to business-touchy data.
- **Identity federation management**
  Organization is the way toward dealing with the trust connections set up past the inward system limits or managerial area limits among particular associations. A league is a relationship of associations that meet up to trade data about their clients and assets to empower joint efforts and exchanges (e.g., offering client data to the associations' advantages frameworks overseen by an outsider supplier). League of characters to specialist co-ops will support SSO to cloud administrations.
- **Centralization of authentication (authN) and authorization (authZ)**
  A focal verification and approval framework reduces the requirement for application designers to construct custom validation and approval highlights into their applications. Moreover, it advances a free coupling design where applications become sceptic to the confirmation strategies and approaches. This methodology is additionally called an externalization of authN and authZ from applications.

Access Control

Access control is a key part of data security that is straightforwardly attached to the essential attributes, for example, privacy, honesty and accessibility. Distributed computing specialist organizations ought to give the accompanying fundamental functionalities from the viewpoint of access control:

- Control access to the administration highlights of the cloud dependent on the predetermined approaches and the degree of administration bought by the client.

- Control access to a shopper's information from different buyers in multi-inhabitant situations.
- Control access to both normal client works and special regulatory capacities.
- Maintain exact access control arrangement and upto date client profile data.

Access control models can be traditionally categorized into three types:

- Discretionary
- Mandatory
- Role-based

In the discretionary access control (DAC) model, the proprietor of the item chooses its entrance consents for different clients and sets them as needs be. The UNIX working framework is an old-style model for optional access control model. For instance, the subject (i.e., proprietor of an item) can indicate what authorizations (read/compose/execute) individuals in a similar gathering may have and furthermore what consents all others may have. DAC models are normally utilized uniquely with heritage applications and will acquire significant administration overhead in the advanced multi-client and multi-application condition, normal for conveyed frameworks, for example, cloud.

The Mandatory Access Control (MAC) models dynamic the requirement for asset client mapping and henceforth are progressively versatile for appropriated frameworks, contrasted with DAC models. The Macintosh model is regularly utilized in staggered security frameworks. Here, the entrance consents are chosen by the chairman of the framework, and not by the subject. In a staggered MAC model, each subject just as item is related to a security level of order (e.g., Unclassified, Classified, Secret and Top Secret). The Bell LaPadula model suggests the no read-up rule and no-record rule for keeping up classification of data. The Biba model suggests the no-review, no-read-down and no-execute-up-or-down rules for keeping up the honesty of data.

In a Role-Based Access Control model (RBAC), a client approaches an item dependent on his/her allotted job in the framework. Jobs are characterized dependent on work capacities. Authorizations are characterized on work authority and obligations of the activity. Procedure on the item is conjured dependent on the authorizations. RBAC models are more adaptable than the optional and obligatory access control models, and increasingly appropriate for use in distributed computing conditions, particularly when the clients of the administrations can't be followed a fixed identity. The connection among clients and assets is dynamic in the cloud, and specialist co-ops and clients are commonly not in a similar security area. Identity-based security (e.g., optional or required access control models) can't be utilized in an open distributed computing condition, where every asset hub may not be natural, or even don't have any acquaintance with one another. For instance, it tends to be seen that clients of a cloud, particularly at the SaaS level access the administrations through the Internet by different methods, for example, cell phone, scratch pad or PDA; henceforth, it is preposterous to expect to distinguish the clients by fixed IP addresses. In such circumstances, one can't utilize the customary firewalls to channel parcels dependent on fixed IP locations of clients. In a cloud, clients are ordinarily recognized by their qualities or attributes and not by predefined personalities. Along these lines, one needs unique access control to accomplish cross-area validation.

For both the grid computing and cloud computing standards, there is a typical should have the option to characterize the techniques through which purchasers find, solicitation, and use assets gave by outsider focal offices, and furthermore actualize profoundly equal and conveyed calculations that execute on these assets. A grid could ordinarily contain process, storage and system assets from various topographically dispersed associations, and these assets are regularly viewed as heterogeneous with dynamic accessibility and limit. The two essential worries for lattice were interoperability and security, as assets originate from various regulatory areas with shifting worldwide and neighbourhood asset utilization strategies, just as various equipment and programming setups and stages. Most frameworks utilize a clump booked register model with appropriate approaches set up to implement the recognizable proof of legitimate client accreditations under which the group employments will be run for bookkeeping (e.g., the quantity of processors required, length of allotment, and so on) and security purposes.

Trust, Reputation, Risk

Right now, talk about existing trust systems in the cloud. From the conversation, we will see that every one of the systems tends to one part of trust however not others. Reputation based Trust and Reputation are connected, yet unique. Fundamentally, trust is between two elements; yet the Reputation of an element is the amassed assessment of a network towards that substance. Generally, an element that has high Reputation is trusted by numerous elements in that network; a substance, who needs to make trust judgment on a trustee, may utilize the Reputation to ascertain or evaluate the trust level of that trustee. Reputation frameworks are broadly utilized in web-based business and P2P systems. The Reputation of cloud administrations or cloud specialist co-ops will undoubtedly affect cloud clients' decision of cloud administrations; subsequently, cloud suppliers attempt to manufacture and keep up higher Reputation. Normally, Reputation based trust goes into the vision of making trust judgment in distributed computing. Reputation is commonly spoken to by a far-reaching score mirroring the general conclusion or few scores on a few significant parts of execution. It is ridiculous to solicit an enormous number from cloud clients to rate a cloud administration or specialist organization against a huge arrangement of mind boggling and fine-grained criteria. The Reputation of a cloud specialist organization mirrors the general perspective on a network towards that supplier, along these lines it is progressively valuable for the cloud clients (for the most part singular clients) in picking a cloud administration from numerous alternatives without specific necessities. Reputation might be useful when at first picking a help, however is lacking a while later. Specifically, as a client picks up involvement in the administration, the trust put on that administration meeting execution or dependability necessities will advance dependent on that experience. SLA check based "Trust, however ever confirm" is a word of wisdom for managing the connections between cloud clients and cloud specialist organizations. Subsequent to building up the underlying trust and utilizing a cloud administration, the cloud client needs to confirm and rethink the trust. A help level understanding (SLA) is a lawful agreement between a cloud client and a cloud specialist organization. In this manner, nature of administration (QoS) observing and SLA confirmation is a significant premise of trust the board for distributed computing. Various models that get trust from SLA check have been proposed. A significant issue is that SLA centers on the noticeable components of cloud administration execution, and doesn't address undetectable components, for example, security and protection. Another issue is that many cloud clients do not have the capacity to do fine-grained QoS checking and SLA confirmation all alone; an expert outsider is expected to offer these types of assistance. In a private cloud, there might be a cloud dealer or a trust authority, which is trusted in the trust space of the private cloud; so the trusted agent or trust authority can give the clients in the private cloud the administrations of QoS observing and SLA confirmation. In a hybrid cloud or inter-cloud, a client inside a private cloud may at present depend on the private cloud trust position to lead QoS checking and SLA confirmation; notwithstanding, in an open cloud, singular clients and some little associations without specialized capacity may utilize a business proficient cloud substance as trust merchant.

Trust as a Service

We have just noticed the requirement for utilizing outsider experts for QoS checking and SLA confirmation. Autonomous evaluation has utility in different parts of distributed computing, too. RSA declared the Cloud Trust Authority (CTA) as a cloud administration, called Trust as a Service (TaaS) to give a solitary point to arranging and overseeing security of cloud administrations from numerous suppliers. The underlying arrival of the CTA incorporates: personality administration, empowering single sign-on among different cloud suppliers, and consistence profiling administration, empowering a client to see the security profiles of numerous cloud suppliers against a typical benchmark. The CTA is an instrument concentrated on cloud trust the executives, and is created from RSA's way of thinking of trust = perceivability + control. As a cloud-based apparatus, the CTA could to a great extent rearrange cloud clients' trust the executives. Be that as it may, a cloud client should in any case make trust judgment about the cloud administration statements gushed in the CTA, in light of the fact that those attestations were made by cloud specialist co-ops themselves. Above all, a cloud client needs to pass judgment on the trustworthiness of the CTA in job as a middle person. The fundamental issue of any TaaS component is about what is the premise of the trust connection between cloud clients and those business trust agents.

Risk

One of the issues that emerge with the selection of cloud administrations is the loss of administration. In any case, there should be an away from of security prerequisites for administrations and information that are facilitated in the cloud. We additionally need to ensure that our cloud arrangement sticks to laws and guidelines as pertinent to our association. There likewise should be an away from of obligations between the cloud customer and the cloud supplier. Some portion of this could be recorded inside an assistance level understanding. We need to think about the disappointment of separation between cloud occupants. With multitenancy, assets are shared on the cloud supplier organize. So we have to guarantee that the cloud supplier is finding a way to guarantee disconnection of system traffic, application occurrences, and virtual machines.

Another risk that we face with cloud selection is seller lock-in. This is the place we have a reliance on a cloud supplier. So we have to have an arrangement B, a leave technique, so that if a seller leaves business or if a portion of the information facilitated at the merchant is subpoenaed by a remote government law authorization organization, at that point we should have the option to go to another cloud supplier or to have benefits by and by on-premises. This must be represented so when we have to do it, we have an arrangement set up, and we can do it rapidly with an insignificant interruption to the business. At that point there's the treatment of security occurrences. It's truly out of our control. The identification revealing and consequent administration of security in any event to a limited extent falls on the cloud specialist organization.

We should be caused mindful of how this will to be finished. What's more, if there is an interface where we can at any rate see recognized security episodes identified with our cloud tenure, we have to comprehend what that is. For perceivability, we have to guarantee that the cloud specialist organization is straightforward about their administration and operational issues identified with cloud occupants. The administration interface that we use for cloud administrations, and announcing should be made sure about. So we have to ensure that it doesn't utilize a module in the program, for instance, that has known vulnerabilities. We additionally need to ensure that the correspondence occurs over HTTPS and not simply

HTTP. Information should be ensured. Delicate information maybe may be named so clients with coordinating names would approach that kind of information. We need to consider information misfortune or information that is out of reach because of a system blackout or an issue at the cloud supplier server farm. So administration coherence is significant. A great deal of this sort of data will be accessible in the administration level understanding between the cloud client and the cloud supplier. There's additionally the chance of malevolent conduct at the cloud specialist organization. Preferably, intensive historical verifications will be led for representatives that work at cloud supplier server farms. Also, now and again, we may have the option to demand the certifications and data about cloud security supplier server farm staff. We have to consider how information gets demolished when it's facilitated in the cloud. Frequently with numerous open cloud suppliers, when information is erased, that region is set apart as promptly accessible to be composed over, and it could even be apportioned to other cloud inhabitants.

Summary

This chapter conferred about the security elements of cloud. As more and more organizations following the cloud so it has become a concern of importance to secure the organization data in public clouds. Hence, the techniques related to infrastructure, data and access control has been briefly discussed in this part.

References

1. Naveed, Muhammad, Dynamic Searchable Encryption via Blind Storage, IEEE Symposium on Security and Privacy, 2014.
2. Proceedings of the 6th International Conference on Security of Information and Networks, Pages 321-325, November 2013, https://doi.org/10.1145/2523514.2527013.
3. P. Mell, What's Special about Cloud Security?, IT Professional, Vol. 14, No. 4, Pages 6-8, 2012, DOI: 10.1109/MITP.2012.

8

Planning and Disaster Recovery in Cloud Computing

Learning Objectives

- To familiarize with the disaster recovery in cloud computing
- To understand disaster recovery plan
- To identify the various disaster recovery solution in cloud

Quick improvement in cloud computing is influencing more enterprises to utilize assortment of cloud administrations. Business is utilizing cloud computing condition to store the information. The cloud computing condition gives perfect answer for information reinforcement, information the board, and information recuperation in case of disasters. It enables the organization's information and applications to flawlessly dwell on remotely found servers that are associated with the system. It likewise gives quick restoration and multi-site accessibility of the product makes less expensive.

Disasters, either natural or manmade, can prompt costly assistance interruption. Two diverse disaster recovery (DR) models can be utilized to anticipate disappointment in a system or CSPs: Traditional and cloud-based help models. Traditional disaster recovery draws near, including week by week and day by day information reinforcements and the presumption that the system registering foundation can be rapidly reconstructed after a disaster have demonstrated lacking over and over. Organizations have moved to the utilization of web applications for deals, client care, production network the board, medicinal services therapeutic records, constant monetary records and other exchange-based applications. A large number of these exchanges would be hard to recover should the organization need to move back to a past variant of a database. In any event, when log records can be utilized to make up for lost time a database duplicate with all exchanges, the procedure relies upon gifted organization labourers who probably won't be accessible to carry out the responsibility.

Disaster Recovery

The term disaster recovery is utilized to depict procedures to guarantee information is moved to a substitute site and an arrangement for restoring the system processing condition exists paying little mind to how tedious, yet for the most part inside days/weeks. Business Continuity will be utilized to depict a procedure where the information and applications can be immediately re-established (minutes/hours), disposing of the time hole in the Disaster Recovery process; henceforth, the name Business Continuity. The business procedure necessities for Disaster Recovery and Business Continuity are commonly characterized on two scales:

Recovery time objective (RTO): The objective for restoring a working system registering condition
Recovery point objective (RPO): The time when information can be recouped (e.g., to the last exchange, starting the previous evening, starting a week ago, and so on.)

The two scales are significant contemplations when evaluating whether an innovation procedure for disaster recovery or business continuity is meeting business process necessities, and distributed computing improves the financial aspects of accomplishing different levels on the two scales.

DR components must have five necessities for an effective execution:

- Have to limit RPO and RTO
- Have a negligible impact on the ordinary framework activity
- Must be geologically isolated
- Application must be re-established to a predictable state
- Must ensure security and privacy

Objectives of Disaster Recovery Plan

There are five objectives for the DR plan:

- Have to restrict RPO and RTO
- Have an insignificant effect on the normal system action
- Must be topographically segregated
- Application must be restored to an anticipated state
- Must guarantee security and protection

Disaster Recovery Requirements

This explains key features for effective cloud service when disaster occurs.

- **Recovery point objective**: Greatest time span assumed for information misfortune when a disaster happens is determined RPO. The necessary RPO is commonly a business choice for certain applications definitely no information can be lost (RPO=0), requiring constant synchronous replication to be utilized, while for different applications, the worthy information misfortune could extend from a couple of moments to hours or even days. The recovery point goal distinguishes how much information you are willing to lose in case of a disaster.
- **Recovery time objective**: It is an estimation of time upto which it can withstand and take back to the framework when a disaster happens. It might be minutes, hours, and days. It might likewise incorporate location of disappointment and planning required servers at reinforcement site to instate an application which is hindered in center of execution. The recovery time goal distinguishes how much personal time is adequate in case of a disaster.
- **Performance**: To make DR administration helpful execution is to be ensured under disappointment free activity by utilizing synchronous replication of use to the reinforcement site and complete the presentation of use to prepare it to utilize.
- **Consistency**: The application which is taken reinforcement when disaster happened ought to be duplicated on same site after leeway of disaster at the predictable state. DR component is valuable to take reinforcement when disaster happens.

Disaster Recovery Challenges

In this section we investigate some common challenges of DR in cloud environments.

- **Dependency**: One of the detriments of cloud administrations is that clients don't have control of the framework and their information. Information reinforcement is on premises of specialist co-ops too. This issue makes reliance on CSPs for clients, (for example, associations) and furthermore loss of information on account of calamity will be a worry for the clients.

- **Cost**: It is clear that one of the principle variables to pick cloud as a DR administration is its lower cost. In this way, cloud specialist organizations consistently look for less expensive approaches to give recuperation systems by limiting various sorts of cost.
- **Failure detection**: Failure location time unequivocally influences on the framework vacation, so it is basic to recognize and report a disappointment as quickly as time permits for a quick and right DR.
- **Security**: As referenced previously, DR can be made essentially or can be human-made. Digital fear based oppression assault is one of human-made catastrophes which can be practiced for some reasons. For this situation, assurance and recuperation of significant information will be a primary objective in DR plans adjacent to of framework reclamation.
- **Replication**: Latency DR systems depend on replication strategy to make reinforcements. In this way, exchanging off between cost, execution of the framework and furthermore replication dormancy is a verifiable test in cloud catastrophe arrangements.
- **Data storage**: Business database stockpiling is one of the issues of endeavors which can be illuminated by cloud administrations. By expanding of cloud utilization in business and market, ventures need to capacity colossal measure of information on cloud-based stockpiles
- **Lack of redundancy**: When a calamity occurs, essential site winds up inaccessible and auxiliary site must be enacted. For this situation, there is no capacity to synchronize or async replication in a reinforcement site yet information and framework states just can be put away locally.

Disaster Recovery Solutions

In this segment, we will talk about some DR arrangements which have been proposed to defeat the issues and difficulties in cloud-based DR.

- **Local backup**: A Linux box can be sent in favor of clients to make control of information and to get reinforcement of the two information or even total application. Neighborhood stockpiling can be refreshed through a verified channel. By this strategy, movement between cloud specialist organizations and furthermore relocation between open to private, and private to open is conceivable. In case of a debacle, nearby reinforcement can give the administrations that were served by the specialist organization.

- **Geographical redundancy and backup (GRB)**: Although geological repetition can be utilized in conventional model, however it is costly and excessively expensive. Two cloud zones have a replication of one another. In the event that one zone ends up down, at that point another zone will be on and give the administrations. There is a module that screens the zones to identify catastrophe. Essential zone has a functioning burden balancer to demand additional assets or even discharged unused assets. Second zone additionally has an aloof burden balancer.

- **Between private cloud storage (IPCS)**: This methodology was proposed for cloud information stockpiling. As per Storage Networking Industry Association (SNIA), in any event three reinforcement areas are essential for business information stockpiling. Clients' information ought to be put away in three distinctive land areas: Servers, Local reinforcement server (LBS) and remote reinforcement server (RBS). The private clouds are set up for any endeavors comprise a few servers and a LBS; and furthermore a between private cloud stockpiling is made in an open cloud comprises the RBSs to be shared between open clouds. This model gives correspondence capacity to reinforcement areas to build information mix.

- **Resource management**; Heterogeneous clouds comprise various equipment and programming, for example, half and half stockpiling and assorted circles. In cloud-based ventures, whole business information is put away in the cloud stockpiling. Thus, information security, wellbeing and recuperation are basic in these situations. Information in peril is the information which has been prepared at the essential host however er has not occurred in the reinforcement have yet. It is important to utilize upgraded innovation for information recuperation away clouds.

- **Secure-distributed data backup (SDDB)**: An inventive strategy has been introduced in (Ueno et al., 2010) to ensure information in case of calamity. The information security method has six phases:

- **First information encryption**: Data must be scrambled subsequent to getting into a server farm.
- **Spatial scrambling**: By a spatial scrambling calculation, the request for information records is changed.
- **Fragmentation, duplication**: Data documents are isolated into certain parts and these sections are copied as far as administration level understanding.
- **Second encryption**: Fragments are scrambled again with an alternate key.
- **Shuffling and distribution**: In the last stage, sections are circulated utilizing a rearranging technique into unused memory limits.
- **Transferring metadata to reinforcement server**: Metadata including encryption keys, rearranging, discontinuity and circulate data is sent to a supervisory server. In the event that a fiasco occurs, the supervisory server will accumulate all data from appropriated gadgets and performs decoding (second), sort and union, opposite spatial scrambling and unscrambling (first), individually.
- **Pipelined replication**: This replication procedure means to increase both the presentation of async replication and the consistency of synchronize replication. In a state of harmony replication, handling can't proceed until replication is totally completed at the reinforcement site. While, in async replication, in the wake of putting away information in the neighborhood stockpiling the procedure can be begun. The outcome can be answered to the customer, and afterward the composes are recreated to the reinforcement site in an age. Pipelined replication performs replication and procedure in parallel as in the accompanying situation.
- **Scale up/down**: Sometimes, performing capacities with high need can diminish cash misfortune or even increment the income in case of a debacle. Need of administration can be characterized by some various highlights, for example, administration level understanding, and the measure of income and pressing needs? After a catastrophic event happens in a zone, cloud specialist organizations are looked with flooding administration demands. For this situation, specialist organizations need to deal with their existent clients' administrations and

furthermore handle new client demands. Specialist co-ops must fulfil existent clients and should serve to new clients however much as could be expected.

- **Dual-role operation**: In this strategy each host can work as the essential host for certain applications and can likewise be the reinforcement have for some different applications. In this engineering, customers send their solicitations to the reinforcement have first; at that point the reinforcement host transmits those solicitations to essential host. Subsequent to handling, essential host sends a log to the reinforcement lastly answer to the customers. At the point when a disappointment occurs, the essential host winds up inaccessible and reinforcement host needs to deal with the solicitations of the bombed host. Notwithstanding, this system can't ensure a decent assistance reclamation without anyone else's input, since reinforcement site must share the assets between its very own solicitations and diverted solicitations.

Summary

Disaster recovery is a relentless issue in IT stages. This issue is more pivotal in distributed computing, since Cloud Service Providers (CSPs) need to offer the types of assistance to their clients regardless of whether the server farm is down, because of a disaster. This chapter gives an idea about disaster recovery concepts in the cloud environments.

References

1. Caraman, M. C, Moraru, S. A, Dan, S, Grama, C, Continuous Disaster Tolerance in the IaaS Clouds, 13th IEEE International Conference on Optimization of Electrical and Electronic Equipment, Pages 1226-32, 2013, http://dx.doi.org/10.1109/OPTIM.2012.6231987.
2. Regis J. Bates, Disaster Recovery Planning: Networks, Telecommunications, and Data Communications, McGraw-Hill, 1992.
3. Zhang Jian-hua, Cloud Computing-based Data Storage and Disaster Recovery, Future Computer Science and Education, 2011.
4. Guster, D, Lee, O. F, Enhancing the Disaster Recovery Plan Thr-

ough Virtualization, Journal of Information Technology Research, 4(4), Pages 18-40, 2011, http://dx.doi.org/10.4018/jitr.2011100102.

9

Setting Up Own Cloud

Learning Objectives

- Understanding various open source tools
- To learn migration of data to cloud
- To give an insight of integration of public and private data

Open Source Tools

Open source innovation has been powering the development of internet providers for a considerable length of time. Initially, open source alluded to a particular way that product engineers structured PC programs. Open source programming is available to anybody and based on a code that clients can view, change, and offer autonomously. Not just has this methodology encouraged more cooperation inside the registering network, yet it has likewise widened the extent of different innovations like distributed computing.

Today, open source tech has become a focal aspect of cloud the board for some clients around the globe. Here are a couple of the best open source apparatuses that your association can use for better cloud the executives:

Apache CloudStack

Intended for use Infrastructure as a Service (IaaS) stages, Cloud-Stack makes it simpler to dispatch and oversee virtual machines in the cloud. Both open and private cloud specialist co-ops utilize this product to streamline cloud the board for their occupants.

CloudStack envelops a whole suite of highlights that clients need inside an IaaS cloud. Not exclusively does the stage enable associations to oversee clients and records, however it additionally conveys key Network-as-a-Service capacities and top-line security. With extra concentration in such territories as outstanding task at hand administration and sending, CloudStack makes it simple for cloud clients to arrangement and design all components of their IaaS mists. Inside this condition, the product enables clients to convey new virtual servers and stop occurrences whenever.

The adaptability of CloudStack bolsters progressively productive application advancement at the endeavor level. With new virtual servers accessible readily available, associations can undoubtedly create and test new applications.

Docker

Docker is the most popular of all open source compartment devices available today. Docker enables clients to merge programming into littler compartments that they would then be able to run as virtual machines. This is a jump forward from increasingly conventional virtualization stages, which expend bigger volumes of assets to virtualize whole PC frameworks. With a compartment, just the working framework (OS) is virtualized, which is progressively proficient and considers more applications to run on a solitary server. Also, Docker has propelled a suite of instruments that help clients with holder the board. With Machine, they can arrangement new holders easily and incorporate them with other open-source stages. Swarm encourages handle issues identified with holder bunching. Form enables clients to consolidate unique compartments from at least one stage, helping them cooperate.

OpenStack

OpenStack is open-source programming that supports the improvement and the executives of both open and private cloud situations. It gives a solitary dashboard through which cloud clients can administer all their process, systems administration, and capacity parts without a moment's delay.

OpenStack enables clients to send other open source advancements alongside it or run it close by big business programming. In that capacity, associations can use its abilities to mechanize basic procedures, for example, web frontend, remaining task at hand provisioning, shared administrations, and then some. Generally, OpenStack enables executives to oversee assets all the more proficiently. Like other open source stages, it is totally adjustable relying upon the novel needs of every client.

Apache Mesos

Apache Mesos addresses the full extent of cloud framework, enabling associations to all the more effectively oversee open, private, or cross breed cloud conditions. The stage can likewise fuse on-premises equipment, which empowers cloud clients to regard their whole computerized condition just as it is situated on one PC.

Advertised as an appropriated frameworks piece, Mesos gives applications application programming interfaces (APIs) for asset the board. In addition, it interfaces applications to a scheduler that all the more equally disperses load adjusts over the whole cloud condition. With the capacity to scale to 10,000s of hubs, Mesos supplements the prerequisites of disseminated databases and applications. Mesos additionally flaunts high adaptation to internal failure, in this manner ensuring high accessibility in any event, during framework overhauls. Likewise, the stage is improved for use with any cloud supplier's condition and in any working framework.

Envoy

Envoy is an edge and administration intermediary intended for single administrations and applications, while likewise flaunting capacities for greater structures. Lyft structured this open-source instrument with inheritance advances, for example, equipment load balancers and NGINX, as a top priority. This establishment empowered the organization to build up a C++ circulated intermediary that runs close by every application and digests the system. The outcome is more noteworthy discernibleness.

For example, Envoy influences out-of-process engineering to work pair with any application language. Backing for HTTP/2 and RCP, just as cutting edge load adjusting highlights make this stage a perfect fit for associations that depend on cloud microservices.

Envoy has become such a mainstream open source instrument for cloud the executives that probably the biggest cloud suppliers, including Amazon Web Services, depend on it. It is additionally a focal feature of Kubernetes organizations around the world.

How to build Private Cloud using Open Source Tools

Eucalyptus

Eucalyptus stands for Elastic Utility Computing Architecture for Linking Your Program To Useful System. It is open source software that was developed by University of California-Santa Barbara for Cloud Computing to implement Infrastructure as a Service. In early 2008, it become the first open source software which is compatible with Amazon Web Service API for deploying On-premise private cloud .Amazon Web Service (AWS) is one of the major players for providing Infrastructure As A Service. They have two popular services Elastic Compute Cloud (EC2) and Simple Storage Service (S3). Eucalyptus provides an EC2 -compatible cloud Computing Platform and S3-compatible Cloud Storage thus its services are available through EC2/S3 compatible APIs.

Eucalyptus can leverage a heterogeneous collection of virtualization technologies within a single cloud, to incorporate resources that have already been virtualized without modifying their configuration. Eucalyptus has five high-level components:

Cloud controller (CLC): It is the entry point into the private cloud for end user, project managers, developers and administrator. It also helps in manage virtualized resources.
Walrus: It implements bucket-based storage, which is available inside and outside the cloud system. It is the storage system, which allow user to store data, organized as bucket and object, it is also used to create, delete, and list buckets.
Cluster controller (CC): It executes on a machine that has network connectivity to the machines that are running on Node Controller and Cloud Controller. It manages the Virtual Machine (VMs) Network. All node controllers associated with a single CC must be in the same subnet.
Storage controller (SC): It provides block-level network storage including support for Amazon Elastic Block Storage (EBS) semantics.
Node controller (NC): It is installed in each compute node to control Virtual Machine activities, including the execution, inspection, and termination of VM instances.

OpenStack

In July 2010, OpenStack was announced and the initial contributes of it are NASA and Rackspace. It is the fastest growing free open source software. Rackspace contributed their Cloud Files platform (code) to power the Object Storage part of the OpenStack, while NASA contributed their Nebula platform (code) to power the Compute part.

OpenStack is a collection of open source software project that developers and cloud computing technologist can use to setup and run their cloud compute and storage infrastructure. Its services are available through Amazon EC2/S3 compatible APIs and hence the client tools written for AWS can also be used with OpenStack. It consists of three core software projects:

- OpenStack Compute Infrastructure also called Nova
- OpenStack Object Storage Infrastructure also called Swift
- OpenStack Image Service Infrastructure also called Glance

Nova is the main part of Infrastructure as a service and it is the computing fabric controller for the OpenStack cloud. Enterprises/Organization can use Nova to host and manage their cloud computing systems. Nova manages all the activities that are needed to support life cycle of instances within the open stack. Swift offers a distributed, consistent virtual object container in which lots of data can be store and from which data can be retrieved. It is capable of storing large number of object distributed across nodes. Glance is a lookup and retrieval system for virtual machine images.

OpenNebula

OpenNebula was first established as a research project back in 2005 by Ignacio M. Liorente and Ruben S. Montero. Since its first public release of software in March 2008, it can be primarily used as a virtualization tool to manage virtualized infrastructure in the data center or cluster, which is usually referred as private cloud. It supports hybrid cloud to combine local infrastructure with public cloud-based infrastructure, enabling highly scalable hosting environments. It also support public cloud by providing cloud interfaces to expose its functionality for virtual machine, storage and network management. Its virtual infrastructure interface discloses user and administrator functionality for virtualization, networking, image and physical resource configuration, management etc. OpenNebula cloud infrastructure provides users with an elastic platform for fast delivery and scalability of services to meet dynamic demand of service end-users. All the services are hosted in Virtual Machines (VM) and then submitted, monitored and controlled in the cloud by using the virtual interfaces such as Command Line interface, XML-RPC API, Libvirt virtualization API etc.

Migrating to Cloud

Stage 1: Establish the migration-architect job

Before you start your cloud migration, build up the migration architect job to lead the exertion. The migration architect is a framework architect-level position liable for arranging and finishing all parts of the migration; their centre obligation ought to incorporate characterizing vital refactoring required to make the migration fruitful, structuring techniques for information migration, characterizing cloud-arrangement prerequisites, and deciding migration needs and creation switchover components. Over the span of an enormous migration venture, there are numerous choices and specialized plans that must be made, and having a migration architect who is liable for all parts of the migration is basic to the achievement of the undertaking.

Stage 2: Choose your degree of cloud integration

At the point when you move an application from an on-premise server farm to the cloud, there are two different ways you can relocate your application a shallow cloud integration or profound cloud integration.

For a shallow cloud integration, you move the on-premise application to the cloud, and make no or constrained changes to the servers you launch in the cloud to run the application. Any application changes are sufficiently only to get it to run in the new condition. You don't utilize cloud-one of a kind administration. This model is otherwise called lift-and-move in light of the fact that the application is lifted as seems to be moved, to the cloud flawlessly.

For profound cloud integration, you alter your application during the relocation procedure to exploit key cloud capacities. This may be nothing further developed than utilizing auto scaling and dynamic burden adjusting, or it may be as complex as using serverless registering capacities, for example, AWS Lambda for parts of the application. It may likewise include utilizing a cloud-explicit information store, for example, Amazon S3 or DynamoDB.

One application in one cloud; another application in an alternate cloud. Maybe the least difficult multi-cloud approach runs one lot of utilizations in a single cloud supplier and another set in another. This methodology gives you expanded business influence with different suppliers just as adaptability for where to place applications later on. It additionally gives you a chance to streamline every application for the supplier on which it runs.

Construct your application to be cloud freethinker. Different organizations construct their applications to run on any cloud supplier. With this methodology, you could run your application all the while on different suppliers or split your application load crosswise over them. This model gives you a definitive adaptability in seller arrangements since you can without much of a stretch move loads starting with one cloud supplier then onto the next. The drawback is that you may think that it's hard to utilize the key abilities of each cloud supplier, decreasing the advantages of facilitating your application in the cloud. This methodology may likewise muddle your application-advancement and approval forms.

Stage 4: Establish execution baselines

Baselining is the way toward estimating the current (pre-movement) execution of your application or administration so as to decide whether its future (post-relocation) execution is worthy. Baselines help you decide when your movement is finished and give approval of the post-relocation execution enhancements you anticipated. You can likewise allude to baselines during a cloud movement to analyze any issues that emerge.

Set a pattern metric for each KPI that you've chosen to gauge. Decide to what extent you will gather information to decide the pattern. Picking a short pattern period, (for example, a day) gives you a chance to move quicker, however you chance not gathering an agent execution test. Picking a more extended period to gauge, (for example, a month) clearly takes additional time, however can give increasingly delegate information.

You likewise need to decide whether you need to gather just standard information that is normal or illustrative, or on the off chance that you need to incorporate information gathered over "top" or "basic" periods. For example, in case you're a news site, would you like to gather information over a day with a major news occasion, or would you like to keep away from such days?

Regardless of which information assortment model is fitting for your industry, make certain to obviously characterize what sort of information you're going to gather and for what timeframe.

Stage 6: Prioritize migration segments

You likewise need to choose on the off chance that you will relocate your whole application on the double, or on the off chance that you will move it to the cloud part by segment or administration by administration.

In the first place, recognize the associations between your administrations, and which administrations rely upon what different administrations. For bigger, increasingly complex applications, utilize an observing application, for example, New Relic APM that can utilize administration maps to create reliance graphs. Utilize the reliance outline to choose which parts ought to be relocated and in what request. It frequently bodes well to begin with the administrations that have the least conditions. For this situation, you'll move your most inward administrations first, and afterward catch up with your peripheral administrations, regularly the ones nearest to your clients. The substitute methodology is to begin with the administrations nearest to your clients the most outside administrations so you can control any effect on your clients.

Stage 7: Perform any fundamental refactoring

You might need to do other work on your applications and administrations before you relocate them so they fill in as viably and proficiently in the cloud as would be prudent. For instance, you may need to refactor your application: So it works viably with a variable number of running cases to permit dynamic scaling, possibly setting aside you cash on cloud administration costs. So your asset use can more readily exploit dynamic-cloud capacities, for example, the capacity to powerfully assign and de-apportion assets varying, as opposed to you statically designating them early. To move to a more assistance arranged engineering before the migration, with the goal that you can all the more effectively move singular administrations to the cloud.

Stage 8: Create an information migration plan

Relocating information is perhaps the trickiest piece of a cloud migration. The area of your information can fundamentally affect the exhibition of your application. Moving your information to the cloud when the information get to techniques are still principally on-premises can fundamentally affect execution. Similar remains constant if the information is still on-premise however the administration getting to it lives in the cloud.

Choices for Information Migration

- Using a bi-directional matching up system between your on-reason and cloud databases. When you've moved all purchasers of the information to the cloud, evacuate the on-premise database.
- Use an on-premise database with single direction synchronization to a cloud-based database, and enable buyers to associate just to the on-premise form. At the point when you're prepared, impair access to the on-premise form so the cloud-based rendition turns into the primary database, and empower cloud-based buyer's access to the new database.
- Use a cloud information migration administration, for example, those accessible from Amazon Web Services and Microsoft Azure.

Stage 9: Switch over generation

When and how would you switch over the generation framework from the inheritance on-premise answer for the new cloud adaptation? The appropriate response relies upon the unpredictability and engineering of your application, and particularly the design of your information and data stores.

There are two basic methodologies:

- Do it at the same time? Hold up until you've moved the whole application or administration over to the cloud and approved that it works there, and afterward change traffic from the on-premise stack to the cloud stack.
- Do it a smidgen at once. Move a couple of clients over, test that things are as yet working, and afterward move a couple of more clients. Proceed with this procedure until you've moved every one of your clients to the cloud-based application.

Stage 10: Review application asset portion

Considerably after you've got done with moving everything to the cloud, there are a couple of more interesting points. Most significant is asset streamlining. The cloud is upgraded for dynamic asset assignment, and when you dispense assets (servers, for instance) statically, you're not exploiting the cloud's qualities. As you move into the cloud, ensure your groups have an arrangement for disseminating assets to your application. At the point when you have to dispense extra assets to an application in the cloud, they are generally accessible from the seller in for all intents and purpose any amount in a minute's notification. This implies you can commonly believe that you can scale varying to satisfy need, accepting your groups have the application engineering set up to help dynamic scaling.

Integration of Public and Private Cloud

Associations have opportunity of decision as far as choosing foundation and administrations; however so as to settle on the correct decision it is essential associations have a comprehension of what the business requires and the abilities of existing framework. Regardless of the unpredictability of business prerequisites and the assortment of decisions accessible, it appears that most organizations are settling on comparable decisions and are going to the greater sellers in the market.

As indicated by ongoing exploration from Gartner, Amazon Web Services' piece of the overall industry is multiple times the size of the various cloud merchants joined. Further research from Gartner likewise shows a solid interest is foreseen for a wide range of cloud administrations; with general society cloud administrations advertise conjecture to become 18.5 percent in 2013 to add up to $131 billion.

While actualizing a cloud administrations into their IT framework, associations ought to right off the bat adjust and coordinate their cloud administrations with assets as of now set up. They ought to know that with the correct advancements and stages, and a blend of both people in general and private cloud, their cloud administration ought to be straightforward, flawlessly incorporated, versatile and above all the right model for the business being referred to.

Utilizing a blend of both private and open cloud and review them as one storehouse, will enable an association to apportion their assets and comprehend which ones are savvy.

While associations might be enticed to strip and supplant their open cloud administration as of now set up while executing private cloud into their IT framework, this can be incredibly troublesome to work effectiveness and doesn't enable adaptability to use the administrations as of now set up.

Notwithstanding, all isn't lost. There are innovations available, which can enable an association to bring their current virtualised foundation and administrations on to one stage. These frameworks empower an association to move benefits up or down as they wish and can be included at the associations possess time and claim pace. Without any limitations set up, associations can have control of their information proficiently and successfully, moving it around as their clients see proper.

At the point when frameworks go down associations need to know where their information is and how they can get to it and they are directly in accepting that they need perceivability and control of their assets, to give lucidity and to reduce expenses. They can accomplish this by using advances and stages which permit control and the board through announcing frameworks. These advancements give an unmistakable perspective on where assets are obtained and apportioned and what their identity is gotten to by inside the association. This administration procedure will likewise enable an association to evacuate administrations which are not required, to eventually reduce expenses and increment work productivity.

Summary

This chapter provided an idea about various open source tools in cloud, so that the user can make use of the same according to their requirement. We also provide information regarding data migration to cloud.

References

1. Z. Pantic, M. Babar, Guidelines for Building a Private Cloud Infrastructure, 2012.
2. X. Bai, M. Li, X. Huang, W.T. Tsai, J. Gao, Vee@Cloud: The virtual test lab on the cloud, International Workshop on Automation of Software Test, Pages 15-18, May 2013.
3. O. Sefraoui, M. Aissaoui, M. Eleuldj, Cloud computing migration and IT resources rationalization, International Conference on Multimedia Computing and Systems, Pages 1164-1168, 2014.

10

Future Directions

Learning Objectives

- Give an insight on current trend in cloud
- Discuss the current market trend of cloud as PaaS and SaaS
- Understanding current market in cloud

Cloud Domain and Scope of Work

The enthusiasm for specialists with data on cloud computing is would like to rise exponentially considering the way that a regularly expanding number of associations are executing this advancement. Along these lines, there are different establishments which give cloud computing courses the seeking after up-and-comers. There is no specific ability capability to learn cloud computing. The contender should preferably be from an IT or PC related establishment with the objective that he/she has the general data about PCs and programming. Data on cloud computing fundamentals or any pertinent experience could be an uncommon extra to locate another profession.

Cloud computing contains a couple of occupations. These could be related to the board, IT structures, end customer support, application improvement, business examination, framework, security and web progression. Each activity requires unequivocal aptitudes. Here's an array of the impressive number of aptitudes required to examine the universe of cloud computing.

Cloud computing occupations are on the ascent. As indicated by an ongoing examination, the worldwide cloud computing market is relied upon to ascend to $72 billion by 2015, and around 3 lakh openings for work in India are normal in a similar period.

The jobs in Cloud Computing may go from cloud designers to administrators. Each job contains the information on the cloud computing nuts and bolts and certain area explicit abilities. Here are some of the major cloud computing certifications:

- EMC Cloud Architect (EMCCA)
- EMC Cloud Infrastructure and Services Certification (Associate Level)
- EMC Virtualized Data Center and Cloud Infrastructure Certification (Specialist Level)
- VMware Cloud Certification
- Certificate of Cloud Security Knowledge etc.

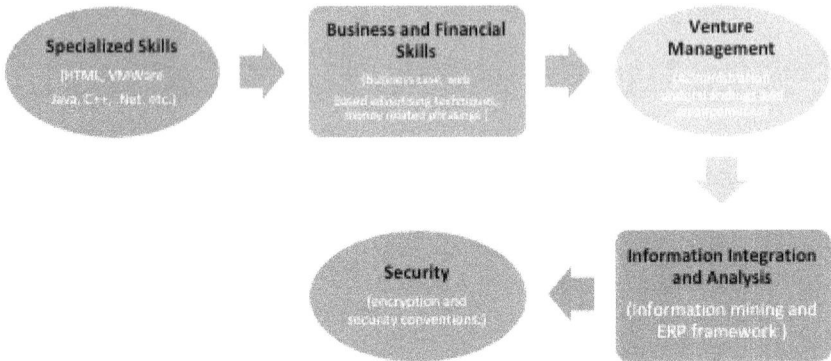

Figure 20. Cloud domain and scope of work.

Cloud as PaaS and SaaS

Cloud can be characterized as the providing segment of computing administrations like storage, organizing, examination, servers, and so on to intrigued organizations over the web. Cloud assists organizations with being savvy, give expedient conveyances, secure information, give an upgraded presentation, be profitable, and so on. It enables substances' to pay just for the administrations they use and in this way, brings operational expense down to help business foundation work all the more expertly.

Presently, a few models can assist you with improving comprehension of where every one of the cloud's administration stage capacities, as follows:

- SaaS - Dropbox, Google Apps

- PaaS - Heroku, Google App motor, OpenShift
- IaaS - Linode, Microsoft Azure, Amazon Web Series, Joyent and so forth

The above gives impact on which all fields this cutting edge business stages work, and here we have inside and out data on their tasks to assist you with choosing which stage is best for your association:

Software as a Service (SaaS)

This is a cloud computing administration which offers organizations access to cloud-based programming. At the point when you select SaaS for your business capacities, you get an application that dwells on the cloud arrange, which can be opened through the web or an API. SaaS doesn't permit to introduce applications on the gadget, be that as it may, stores them on a remote cloud organize. It benefits your organization by decreasing costs and time expended on undertakings like introducing, taking care of, and advancing programming.

Characteristics of SaaS

- Provides applications and programming through a membership model.
- There is no compelling reason to oversee, introduce and overhaul programming.
- Data is secure.
- Resources can be scaled.
- Makes programming and application accessible anyplace just with a web association.
- Hosted on a remote server.
- Managed from one area.

When to Use

- If you need to dispatch your product/application as right on time as could reasonably be expected, SaaS can help.
- Used for assignments which require collaboration.
- Used for applications that need nearness over both web and versatile.

Platform as a Service (PaaS)

This platform assists organizations with getting equipment and programming devices accessible through the web. It gives organizations a cloud situation where clients get the opportunity to create, oversee and convey applications. It stores information for all intents and purposes, besides, offers access to tools that can create, tweak and test applications improving business process administrations.

Characteristics of PaaS

- There is no stress of hidden infrastructure and subsequently, gives sufficient opportunity to concentrate on improvement.
- Integration of web administrations and databases.
- Different clients can get to the equivalent application.
- Automates business approach.
- Less utilization of coding in this way spares time.

When to Use

- When different engineers are working on a similar undertaking, PaaS offers extraordinary speed and even makes your business procedure adaptable.
- Helps to build up possess tweaked application and accordingly can be utilized for custom-form applications' advancement.
- During the time spent improvement and sending of applications, PaaS can decrease costs and can disentangle business challenges.

Trends and Market in Cloud

Only a couple of years back, some industry specialists expelled cloud registering as simply the most recent innovation craze, useful for creating a great deal of buzz however offering minimal handy worth. Today, the cloud has shown up and has been broadly recognized by investigators and organizations the same as a significant power in essentially modifying the whole IT scene, from how server farms are worked, to how programming is conveyed, to how overhauls are taken care of, and past.

Given the imperative job that IT plays in the present business condition, cloud registering is additionally on a very basic level changing the manner in which that organizations work. A huge number of organizations of all sizes in an expansive scope of ventures are using cloud-based programming, stages, and even framework to streamline forms, lower IT multifaceted nature, increase better perceivability, and lessen costs.

With the pace of progress quickening significantly more, what will the eventual fate of cloud registering bring? Here are five cloud processing patterns to watch.

- Adoption of cloud registering will keep on developing quickly
  Unmistakably cloud registering is definitely not a tiny blip on the radar. Truth be told, cloud registering is balanced for emotional development even over the mind boggling gains it has encountered in the course of recent years.
  Today, just about a fourth of organizations as of now use cloud-based applications, and in excess of 10 percent intend to extend their utilization of cloud computing. At the point when estimated in dollars, the development is much all the more striking: In 2008, income from overall cloud administrations was $46.4 billion; in 2013, it is relied upon to reach $150 billion, a hop of a little more than 225 percent.2 Cloud registering is well on its approach to turning into the favoured innovation arrangement model for organizations around the world.
- The eventual fate of cloud registering is portable
  The prominence of cell phones, for example, PDAs and tablets is likewise majorly affecting the business world. Rather than being attached to work areas in an office, the present laborers can utilize their cell phones to carry out their responsibilities whenever from pretty much anyplace.
  The adaptability requested by the portable workforce is one of the key reasons cloud processing is on the ascent. The whenever, anyplace get to that cloud-based applications give is perfect to labourers who are consistently in a hurry. Instead of halting by the workplace to utilize their PCs, representatives can basically sign into an application with a web-empowered gadget like a cell phone or tablet and play out their assignment in the cloud.
  An ever increasing number of organizations understand the accommodation and efficiency advantages of utilizing porta-

ble cordial cloud processing applications to oversee business information. For instance, specialists anticipate that in excess of 33% of business insight usefulness will be devoured through handheld gadgets by 2013.

- The cloud will turn out to be increasingly worldwide
From various perspectives, the cloud is as of now worldwide all things considered, organizations everywhere throughout the world are utilizing cloud-based devices consistently. Be that as it may, as cloud administrations keep on advancing, they will permit an ever-more noteworthy level of correspondence and joint effort crosswise over associations everything being equal. Practically speaking, this will mean more frameworks will have the option to work flawlessly over various areas by giving neighborhood capacities like multi-cash monetary devices and multi-language interfaces, among numerous others.

- Companies become progressively frictionless on account of the cloud
By encouraging access to precise data and making correspondence simpler, the cloud is perfect for separating obstructions, both inside between offices or individual staff individuals or remotely, among clients and client care workers, for instance. At the point when hindrances are expelled, organizations lose the erosion indicates that utilized moderate them down. Mechanized stock chains and dashboards that show constant information are only two instances of cloud-empowered instruments that are on the ascent and making organizations progressively "frictionless."

- Social instruments will carry expanded coordinated effort to the cloud
Cloud-based applications aren't simply more adaptable than customary on location programming; they can be increasingly social as well. For what reason is this so significant? Today, clients hope to have social devices, for example, talk and small scale blogging to improve coordinated effort. As individuals become increasingly acquainted with these devices and begin to favour them to customary apparatuses like email clients will need to utilize them to speak with individual workers, clients, and possibilities.

Cloud programming will progressively go social and will eventually end up being an indispensable business information. Since cloud registering is locally online and updates are consequently turned out to cloud arrangements all the time, it is anticipated that this capacity should advance rapidly.

Summary

All the topics discussed in this chapter have potential impact. The future can be famously difficult to foresee, yet cloud processing is sure to keep significantly affecting business activities.

References

1. R. Buyya, C. S. Yeo, S. Venugopal, Market-Oriented Cloud Computing Vision, Hype, and Reality for Delivering IT Services as Computing Utilities, Proceedings of the 10th IEEE International Conference on High Performance Computing and Communications, Pages 25-27, China, 2008.
2. http://dazeinfo.com/2015/07/01/the-future-of-cloudcomputing-127-billion-market-by-2018-report/
3. Buyya, R, Yeo, C, Venugopal, S, Broberg, J, Brandic, I, Cloud Computing and Emerging IT Platforms Vision, Hype and Reality for Delivering Computing as the 5th Utility, Future Generation Computer Systems, Elsevier, The Netherlands, 25(6), Pages 599-616, 2009.
4. Cloud Computing: IT professionals with multi-cloud skills to have higher demand in 2020, TechGig.

www.ingramcontent.com/pod-product-compliance
Lightning Source LLC
Chambersburg PA
CBHW071227210326
41597CB00016B/1975